PSYCHIC POWER

Answers to all your questions for a
happier money, health and love life

Una Power

Published in 2006
by Maverick House Publishers,
Main Street, Dunshaughlin, Co. Meath.
www.maverickhouse.com
email: info@maverickhouse.com

ISBN 1-905379-07-2

Printed and bound by Mackays of Chatham Ltd.

The paper used in this book comes from wood pulp of managed forests.
For every tree felled, at least one tree is planted, thereby renewing
natural resources.

A CIP catalogue record for this book is available from the British Library.

*This book is dedicated with love
to my husband Martin Dunne.*

Contents

Acknowledgements

I would like to thank several people for their help. Without them this book would not have been written. Thanks to my husband Martin. Thanks also to Mary Sellars and Carmel Farrell for their typing and support. And thanks to all at Maverick House, who had faith in this book, and to Adam Hyland for his helpful suggestions.

Signs of The Zodiac

Sign	Date of Birth	Symbol	Ruling Planet
ARIES	21st Mar - 19th Apr	The Ram	Mars
TAURUS	20th Apr - 20th May	The Bull	Venus
GEMINI	21st May - 20th Jun	The Twins	Mercury
CANCER	21st June - 22nd July	The Crab	Moon
LEO	23rd Jul - 22nd Aug	The Lion	Sun
VIRGO	23rd Aug - 22nd Sep	The Virgin	Mercury
LIBRA	23rd Sep - 22nd Oct	The Scales	Venus
SCORPIO	23rd Oct - 21st Nov	The Scorpion	Mars
SAGITTARIUS	22nd Nov - 21st Dec	The Archer	Jupiter
CAPRICORN	22nd Dec - 19th Jan	The Goat	Saturn
AQUARIUS	20th Jan - 18th Feb	The Water Bearer	Saturn
PISCES	19th Feb - 20th Mar	The Fish	Jupiter

Introduction

I am sitting alone in my small broadcast studio before a single microphone. I am wearing headphones and have one eye on the clock. The minutes are ticking down towards the start of my live two-hour radio show. I am looking through a pile of correspondence, each letter, fax or e-mail containing a listener question and giving their date of birth.

Through the glass panel I can see the crew, heads bent as they take a constant stream of calls from listeners wanting to come on air with me and ask a question of my psychic powers, about some puzzling aspect of their present or future. The show producer is standing up at the control desk checking that the equipment is working. Glancing to her left, she catches my eye and motions to me that she is ready to do a sound check.

Everything is fine. We have our first six callers lined-up and ready to come on air. I check my cards, just an ordinary deck of playing cards, and look through them to make sure they are all there. It's not the same deck as I used when starting the show; there have been many cards used since then. We are into the tenth year of the show. When it started we thought we would be lucky if it lasted six months.

No one dreamt in 1996 that we had started a phenomenon that was to change how the media treated psychic matters. We agreed at the outset that we would set up a psychic radio show where listeners had a chance to ask one question and we would treat the subject, the callers and the listeners seriously and courteously.

The radio station, Dublin's 98FM, loves its listeners and we were to discover that our listeners loved us. They have given us ten years of loyalty and none more so than to the twice weekly programme THE PSYCHIC ZONE.

It's hard to appreciate now in 2006 — when most radio stations have jumped on the 98FM success bandwagon and employ psychics, and umpteen psychic phone-in lines operate all over the country — that we were the first. My first producer, inspired and inspiring woman Tina Convey, was producing a radio first. The steady stream of callers became a deluge and the live show moved at a frantic pace. Up to four crew members manned the phone lines, taking as many as five hundred calls during the show.

Callers wanted to know about their love lives, about their jobs or financial prospects, or maybe about either their own health or the health of someone close to them. One early caller wanted to know if she would ever find the daughter she gave up for adoption. By a remarkable coincidence, a young girl listening in was convinced that our caller was the mother she had been searching for. After careful checking on our part, that girl was proved right and eventually with the assistance of social workers, mother and daughter were re-united.

We grew with the experience our 98FM listeners gave us. Right from the outset we decided that apart from the courtesy and respect we would show our listeners, that I would always tell the truth about what I felt physically and what I saw in the cards I cut.

A few years later I began a slot on a new programme starting on TV3, a morning show called IRELAND AM. That show is another phenomenal success.

My psychic abilities have grown over the years. They were first evident when I was a very young child. My godfather, a merchant seaman, had come to see us when his ship docked in port. As he was leaving I ran out after him to say a special goodbye. Afterwards my mother asked me why I had done that. I told her it was because we would never see him again. He drowned the following week. My mother, a devout Catholic, was disturbed and asked me never to talk like that again. That puzzled me. I was five years old, and to me it was nothing remarkable; it was like having another sort of memory.

* * *

The large black hand on the white clock face is ticking down towards ten o'clock. My producer, Becky Johnson, opens her microphone, her voice sounds in my headphones, 'Twenty seconds to air. First caller on line.' I feel the familiar fizz of excitement in my stomach, a picture of the first caller forms in my mind. Her name, Jessica, is flashing on the monitor. I can sense a neat girl in her late twenties, with an oval face, a good career and unlucky in love.

The big red light comes on in my broadcast studio, my microphone is live and we are ready to go for another two hours in the PSYCHIC ZONE.

Jessica's voice is smooth, cultured but just a shade anxious.

'Will I ever find a soul mate? I never seem to have any luck in love.'

She gives me her date of birth, 15th May. I shuffle her cards and lay them out. Fortunately, Jessica is going to be lucky.

LOVE

Finding And Keeping Your Soul Mate

It's the most frequently asked question on my radio show, on my television slots and in my office when I'm doing a one-to-one personal reading, 'Is there any romance for me?' Women obviously want to be in a relationship with a partner they are physically attracted to and to feel that their partner feels the same way about them. But that's only one part of what women are looking for in a relationship. Over and over they tell me that what they want is to find a partner who is kind, caring and loving, someone they can live with happily and on terms of mutual respect. Sounds easy, doesn't it? Wrong. Loveland is a minefield and goes wrong sometimes. But we women never stop the endless search for that perfect love. Some, but not by any means all women, want their every deepest need fulfilled by a soul mate.

Ideally you want a man to love and be loved by. One who will stand by you at all times, be your best friend, someone you can laugh with, grow old with. You need your man to be strong when you are feeling weak or uncertain, to share with you all the crises that occur in normal life together and give you space to have your own friends, get on in your job and share parenting with if you decide to have children together. Better still, to be a good dad to your children if you come into the relationship with children of your own.

The first question you MUST ask yourself is, 'Can this man take care of himself?' Because if the answer to that is 'no', then there's no possible way he can take care of you. Worse, he'll be a liability if there are children around.

Some signs are better than others at asking this question and facing the truth about the man they've decided to fall in love with. Other signs are an outright disaster zone and lurch from one relationship to another moaning, 'Every relationship I've ever been in ends in failure and yet another loser.'

♎ **LIBRA** is a beautiful sign; stylish, gracious and born to be part of a twosome, but so desperate for a relationship that she will put up with the most atrocious behaviour rather than admit she's backed an unsuitable lover. Libra deserves a soul mate.

In work Libra is cool, shrewd and very successful. She treats her friends very well, is always there for them and absolutely spot on in summing up and weighing up if her best friend's new relationship is going anywhere. She'll be the first to tell a friend if the relationship isn't going to work and why. So why doesn't this work for the Libra lady herself?

Simply put, the Libra lady doesn't believe that she is as beautiful on the inside as she is on the outside. In early childhood she absorbed all the negative messages about herself and allowed the positive ones to skip way over her head. She believes that love has to be suffered for, competed for and won. Poor little Libra never believes that love is her very own life gift. So she takes on a man already flawed in the belief that that's all she can get. She then proceeds to ignore the facts about him, for instance that he has no job, accepts her money to gamble with, expects her to work pay-free hours in his business and entertain his mother for hours because 'dear old mum' bores him too much.

The Libra lady leaps in with all the ready made excuses for her man as long as he looks good, dresses well and is at her side in public. She'll pay for the holidays and show the photos off to the friends telling them all what a good time they had. If he walks out on a job she explains that he was stressed and unappreciated. If he falls in the door three hours late for dinner she excuses him on the grounds that he was led astray by friends — not hers of course.

Wake up Libra; make two lists, one of the facts about his behaviour, then the excuses you make for him. Then burn the excuses list. Look for a mate who loves your soul.

SCORPIO understands more than any other sign the true nature of 'soul mate' and 'soul mating'. You Scorpios are among the most intuitive and psychic of all the signs. You are famed for your sexual magnetism but in your mate you want much more than a good sexual partner. You want and need someone who can explore with you the depths of your sometimes very dark lows and the heights of your wild and wonderful ups. You read character in a split second but take very good care that no-one will get to know you too quickly. You're amazingly tolerant and understanding of human weakness and truly noble in giving full credit for courage, true kindness and unselfishness in a partner.

That's your secret. That's why you, more than any other sign of the zodiac, often find your soul mate. It's because you see right into the soul of a person and see the deepest, darkest recesses and the bright shining lights and then accept the person totally and completely for what they are without attempting to change them in any way whatsoever. For you, a soul mate will go side by side with you through the huge number of emotions you experience all the time. You take a long time to trust a man, and he has to earn that trust, but when it happens, it's total and complete. He might never know it because you don't always show it, but you become absolutely devoted to him, growing closer and happier with each day passing. You know instinctively if he is hiding something and use all your persuasive charm to ferret out the truth. Whatever that truth is you know how to deal with it. Love is what your soul is made of and the mate you put into your heart and soul owns you completely. If your relationship is threatened you'll fight tooth and nail to restore it. You won't give up on it — ever. If he's been unfaithful you'll be deeply, deeply wounded, but you won't give up on him. Once you've found him you'll never want to let him go. You have, undeservedly I think, a reputation for being sex-driven — you aren't, you're love driven — and you have the most fantastic ability to forgive even if it takes you a long time to forget.

Scorpios are amongst the best at keeping their soul mate because there isn't anything you won't do to keep that mate. You have the attitude that the soul is for ever. If there's a row, or a misunderstanding, you clear it up quickly and take the attitude that the problem belongs to yesterday. Tomorrow is a fresh start. You're as attracted by the weakness in your partner as you are by the strengths. That's your particular strength. But you want an equal. If your partner starts the 'ickly-wickly, poor little me's' you snap them out of it very quickly. Your need is for a mate of equal intelligence and emotional capacity to go with and grow with through life's journey.

CAPRICORN ladies — and you are ladies, even as early as eleven, are on the look-out for a type that you can respect. You're looking for a set of qualities you admire rather than questing for a soul mate. You definitely like dignity and stylish dressing and admire a good money maker. For you, very often a man is what he does, or, sometimes, doesn't do for a living. You just can't respect a slob. Love is as much about respect as it is about feeling attracted to a partner. You search for your ideal man and that means he has to meet some pretty high standards. Appearance is important to you and if he has no dress sense, is not immaculate in his hygiene, he doesn't even get a second look from you. Whether he's a bricklayer, bouncer or the boss — you like the boss kind; means he's going places — you want him to achieve his highest work potential. Once you see him trying then you're attracted. You respect hard work, and money honestly earned. You absolutely hate a time-waster, a financial fool and lack of ambition. You're pretty realistic about life, you want the goodies but know they don't grow on bushes and have to be paid for with hard cash. You'd like him to buy you a diamond ring, but would hate it and him if it has to be bought on the credit card.

You want, need and give commitment early on in the relationship. No messers need apply for the position of your husband. You want a secure property, within your financial limits, marriage and children, in that order. You watch out for bad behaviour; it tells you oceans about a man. If his idea of a good time is to get drunk at your sister's wedding and tumble off the bar stool, he'll tumble so far down in your esteem that he's out of sight. You don't do it yourself and expect the same of him. You Capricorns detest and rarely use bad language; it's all part of your high and sound standards. If he loses his job or money you don't expect or encourage him to sit around pitying himself, moaning about life or bad luck. More than any other sign you recognise the essential truth that life is exactly what you make of it. You're a worker, a hard worker and you want a partner to share that with you. You want to live with him in a secure, stable home created by the two of you. If he has an ex, and/or children with an ex, you'll expect him to honour his financial obligations to them. It's a great tribute to you that that bill is factored into your financial planning. God, they say, loves a trier, and so do you, Capricorn lady. In return you'll give him your love, your loyalty and a lifetime commitment.

If it doesn't work out you'll end the relationship smoothly with dignity and scrupulous financial fairness. You aren't greedy and don't want to look for anything that isn't yours by right. But heaven help the man who tries to take more than his fair share.

GEMINI woman — you attract men to you all your life. You adore flirting, chatting and thrive on some very heated debate (notice how cleverly I avoided saying a good old row). You aren't consciously searching for anything except a man with a stimulating mind, plenty to say and a quirky sense of humour. You get chosen. Did you realise that? No? Read on. You are what a lot of men are looking for. You're attractive, vivacious, great with children, very enthusiastic about your work, have loads of friends and are as at home with males as with your female friends. You've got very good social manners and treat everyone, young and old with the same open friendliness. You can get a meal together, decorate the table, open the post, send off a few e-mails, access your messages, return one or two of them, while telling your partner of the funny things that happened to you that day. And that's all within ten minutes of getting in from work. Phew!

You're a hard act to follow. You don't think too far ahead, you're a here and now person. Your home is an easy, carefree place to be in. You're transparent in all your moods, laughing and crying with equal and unaffected ease. You fascinate men of all ages; they can't get enough of you whether you're seventeen or seventy. Building a relationship is something you do without even being aware of it. Men absolutely gag for the combination of qualities leaping out of you. Put the music on, you dance, tell you a sad story, you weep. Hand you a problem and you instantly set about finding the solution. Men want that seemingly carefree attitude of yours combined with your honesty. He'll always know where he stands with you. And with you is where he wants to stand. I've known Gemini women to have as many as two proposals of 'let's do the living together thing' in the same week and be equally surprised by both. If it sounds like fun you'll go for it, with the same swift ease with which you do everything else. You're not searching for love, just finding it in just about everything you do.

Then you move in together, or maybe marry; formal contracts aren't too important to you. Then you begin to discover what your needs are. Maybe he'll not take a fair share of housework and that will cause a few ructions. Maybe he'll leave you to go out six nights on the trot while the baby is teething and you discover that you're feeling unfairly treated. Life's journey is one of constant discovery for you in your relationship. Then you start to make a few rules and announce them to him. If he doesn't agree there's a mini war until he comes round to your way of thinking. You are one of the most brilliant parents in the zodiac but you insist that he does his share, otherwise the unfairness of it all begins to eat away at you.

Although you are the great flirt of the zodiac, you are fundamentally the faithful type. There is an underlying seriousness in your personality. In any case your emotions are so transparent you'd never get away with an affair outside of your relationship, not for long anyway.

If your relationship does end it would be unlikely to be your doing. Although you're relaxed about the formalities of actually being married, you are in heart and soul a faithful wife. So if he wants to leave, you are stunned, deeply hurt and very angry. You may not have consciously thought much about the future but it probably never occurred to you that the two of you wouldn't grow old together. All the rules and social conventions you thought you didn't care about were always there, just beneath the surface, dominating, controlling, and running your life. You won't give up easily and you'll be one of the first to seek counselling. Talking is your strong point and helps you to understand yourself, your motives and his. If he, having chosen you, cheats on you or attempts to desert you, he'll find he has a ferocious reckoning to pay.

With real compassion and from the very best of humanitarian motives you try hard never to involve your children in any dispute you have with your partner. You shield them with the warmth of your love.

A tip! Get married before the domesticity sets in because, without realising it, when you are young you are a born wife and mother.

🦁 **LEO** girls — and you are girls all your lives — your search is for dream love. You get trapped in the headlights of fascination. A man will fascinate you, you become obsessed with him, want him, can't live without him, think about him all the time, dream about him, go off your food. You don't know if he's your soul mate, it's not your sort of thinking. All you know is that you can't live without him. All that can happen within five minutes of meeting him. Something clicks in your mind and he's the ONE, and you can't rest until you have him. Without realising it, you're the lioness hunting once that deep chord has been struck inside you. It wouldn't matter to you if you came from a background of wealth and privilege or he lived in a shabby little bedsit, you wouldn't even think of it, all that matters is the two of you share a life together.

You're demanding of him; his time, his love, his affections, his mind, his body, but you're not that interested in his money or his status. Once your love object returns your feelings you bloom and blossom like some gorgeous exotic flower. If he doesn't return your feelings immediately you'll wait until he does. Love is something that just happens to you, unbidden, unexpected and if his status is unimportant to you, so is his age. Yours is the sort of love that inspired *Wuthering Heights* or *Gone with the Wind*. You're all grand drama, deep passion and unswerving loyalty. That very deep and profound chord that love strikes is your soul. Subconsciously you recognise it and even if, in the eyes of your friends or family, he is unsuitable for you, you know in the very core of you that life is tasteless and colourless without him.

You commit easily and naturally and then expect all you give to the relationship, in both the bed and in the kitchen. Life becomes a beautiful drama featuring the two of you as starring players. What rescues you from living life in the emotional spotlight is your sense of fair play and your appreciation of the absurd. You have a highly developed sense of humour and you can send yourself up in the most delightful way. In love, all that is finest in your creative soul is drawn out. You make a beautiful home and pour so much love into it that the very air you breathe is sweet with it. You want to own him, marry him, live with him and for him. He IS your soul, for him you were created and he for you. If he even looks at another woman a fury is unleashed in you and only your sense of fair play stops you from desperate measures. If you are the one doing the changing you do it with the minimum of fuss and the maximum speed. You take all the lessons you learned from the first marriage or relationship into the next and often more successful one. But divorce or separation is rare in Leo relationships, you'll often marry your childhood sweetheart and the love affair lasts a lifetime.

PISCES — you're so feminine and romantic and in love with being in love. But you're often drawn to macho men who have as much idea of soul mate stuff as Saddam Hussein has about being an agony aunt. You spent so much time dreaming about an old-fashioned courtship, about being treated like a fragile treasure, about the happy nest you and he would share together that you forgot to actually go out there and search for your ideal mate. You know, you've always known what suits you, what your needs are, so why have you so often settled for second best? Could it be that you mixed up sexual attraction with soul mate qualities somewhere along the line? Your love-life brings you as many questions as answers, yet you never give up and that little flame of hope never quite goes out. You are intuitively clear about what sort of man doesn't appeal to you and you don't give that sort of man a second glance or thought. If you follow your intuition it will lead you to your soul mate very quickly. He has to be the one to love you mentally and physically. He must laugh with you, love with you and be prepared to experiment a bit with life.

You crave, need, and deserve the old-fashioned hearts and flowers bit but you also have a deep need for a man to love you and understand you without words. You need him to tune into your soul as you tune into his. You want to make music with him, soul music. Because it feels right, some of you Pisceans will sleep with your man on the first date and then wonder why he either drops you or only has a sexual relationship with you. You need him to understand without having to put it into words that sex for you is only one part of your offering on the sacred altar of love. The right man will understand that. It is part of Piscean karma that a soul mate will always find you. It might even be your first love coming back into your life carrying the flowers you always wanted and asking you, over a candle-lit dinner to marry him. Or, if you divorced him, to marry him again, in white in the chapel, or wherever. Your Piscean is an old and very wise sign and is always rewarded for its undying hope and faithful love.

VIRGO woman has an instinct about that perfect partner, the soul mate with whom you will share your life. On the surface it's a very practical business with the unsuitables not even getting the start and the possibles being scrutinised very carefully. Your mind tells you one thing but your soul knows better. A lot of you Virgoans won't marry until you're in your thirties because you are seeking what you know you're going to find, HIM, the soul mate, the perfect man for you. And the great thing about you Virgo is that you know where to look.

Virgo won't waste her time hanging around bars, discos and nightclubs because her sort of man doesn't go there. She likes her man, the man she'll share her soul with, to be masculine, stable, financially solvent and above all else, conservative. Secretly, she also wants him to be sexually wild and an occasional rebel but she never even admits that to herself. Sensibly, she never rules out the dating.

Virgo lady has the sense to hunt her man on his own territory so she is likely to join a political party, a sports club (that gives her a very good excuse to show off her figure) or maybe join the social club at work. Even when Virgo lady's heart is pumping like mad at the sight of a man she fancies wildly, she won't make a move, or allow him to guess her feelings, until she has found out quite a bit about him. Her practical instinct sends her on a mission to find out where and how he lives, where he works, what his family background is and who his friends are.

The first date, on which she will be impeccably rather than sexually dressed, is definitely an intelligence-gathering foray. She has a list of questions in her head about her soul mate. If his answers are satisfactory she will move onto the next stage when she gently but firmly informs him of her expectations. Stage three of the operation is quite subtle; she watches his actions and logs them into her database. Is he insured? Does he arrive on time for dates? Does he have a regular savings plan? Very importantly, does he respect and honour his relatives? Slip-ups at this early stage won't count against him overly much, as she knows that dealing with the right material, she can mould him into her ideal man.

Virgo wages a fairly lengthy campaign; no losing the head and the heart in a few months when she is dealing with something as important as her life-long marriage. Marriage is for her, and it's for life. But once she has her life booked he will be hugely rewarded with her total commitment to him, his children, his family, his friends (she will, early on in the campaign have weaned him off unsuitable friends). She will love him devotedly and as she relaxes into marriage, be everything the most uninhibited man could ever want in bed. His home will be the well run and peaceful haven he looks forward to returning to after a long hard day. She can and will share her deepest and most intimate thoughts, desires and needs with him. She is the most unlikely candidate in the entire zodiac to have an affair or betray his trust.

It will only go wrong if the list in her head of what she expects from her perfect man expands into the impossible, and she believes that he is not trying hard enough, or is failing her in some way. Then she starts to NAG. It starts with gently nit-picking, then critical lectures, then the final stage, relentless nagging. At this stage he is standing on his head, filling the dishwasher, and promising to work harder, correct the children and make more money simultaneously.

If she is going down the sensible route, Virgo lady will back off, redesign the perfection model in her head and learn to settle for less than perfection.

Her saving grace is her sense of justice and humour, and her great abiding need to save and keep her marriage.

ARIES girl carried an image from early childhood of a big strong man who would march at her side through life, loving her, protecting her and evolving with her. She is a love kaleidoscope of furious energy, passionate sex, frank talk and the need for constant change. Although she talks left wing and is vehement about the need for social change to protect the poor and underprivileged, she privately admires high status and the type of man who wants to be the best journalist, plumber, jockey, builder or whatever. She's not too bothered about his appearance; it's his energy and quick mind that appeals to her. She isn't looking for an opposite or a complementary in her soul mate but a mirror image of herself.

Contrary to popular astrological opinion she rarely goes hunting for her man. Rather, as she crosses the threshold of a room, or bar, or office she senses his presence, turns to look at him and, as she advances towards him, decides that this is her man, the man she has subconsciously sought since early childhood. She gives him her hand and a radiant smile. Instantly in her gestures, her words, all all her unspoken communications, she is yielding, possessing and deeply intimate. They will be a couple in those first few moments as though they had been so for a hundred years.

If she has got it wrong — which would be very, very rare — and discovered that her entrance into his life was greeted with squeaks and twitters and an apologetic backing away, she would most likely aim a healthy athletic kick at his hind quarters, then move cheerfully and unashamedly away, dismissing him and her error without concern.

Aries woman never, ever plays coy games. She doesn't have time. She is too busy with a hundred other things. She is active, direct and an emotional breath of fresh air. She wants the status of marriage, expects it as the natural outcome of her relationship with her soul mate, but she is not in any great hurry. She will live quite contentedly with her partner until marriage, because from the moment of meeting, she cannot live without him. She needs him mentally and physically all the time. If her family or friends don't like or approve of him, she will drop them. They don't meet the needs of her soul, he does. Her success lies in that knowledge of herself. The hideous fate of being torn between disapproving family and friends and her soul mate is never Aries' lot. There is in her mind no choice at all, her man is her life, her reason for living.

There is no doubt she is one of the most popular signs in the zodiac with heaps of friends, invited to just about everything and a work and social diary so full it would take someone with ten times her considerable energy to fulfil, but she is not deeply confiding. She has a million hopes, fears, dreams and thoughts that never get told until she meets her soul mate. Then it all pours out. He becomes the recipient of her very essence, her inspiration.

She is completely exclusive to him and expects the same from him. Once he commits to her she won't want him socialising without her, living in his family's pocket. If he visits his family she will expect to go with him. If she senses that he is losing interest in her sexually she will resent him. If, on the other hand, she loses sexual interest they stand in danger of drifting apart. Most Arians are capable of an active and varied sex life right into their eighties — and beyond.

TAURUS women are not particularly money-driven yet they often find a soul mate in places or institutions connected with money. The bank, the financial institution, the bookies office, the farmers' mart. She knows that if he handles money well and wisely, that's the way he handles life. She can easily fall in love and find sexual enchantment in the way the insurance salesman sells her a policy, or the way the bank official describes that loan she is seeking to modernise her kitchen. If the car salesman is efficient enough, what started as a car selling or buying transaction can turn into a real love interest. But Taurus is one of the most complex of the signs of the zodiac for she has the brain of the sturdy farmer and the heart and soul of the artist. She looks deceptively simple in her well-tailored clothes, her clear skin and well-groomed hair, with elegant manners and down to earth talk.

Without giving too much away, she expects her love to understand her huge need for physical love and reassurance. She is naturally attracted to extreme good looks, that's her artistic nature, but coarseness of any sort offends her soul. Her soul, her connection with a higher spirituality, is something of which she has been aware all her life. She isn't the slightest bit turned on by a macho display of bad language or sexist jokes. They disgust her soul.

She talks well, and can fascinate with her very wide knowledge. Her passion about her convictions is endearing; she is almost child-like in her earnestness. She can follow the threads of the most complex arguments and has a devastatingly accurate memory. So if she catches her soul mate out in a lie she can pounce with the speed and ferocity of a mother puma. Once a doubt sets in, it leads her to query every aspect of the relationship. She wants what she offers her soul mate — purity of soul. She can forgive him the odd murder or bank raid, once he has told her the truth.

She will never discuss him or his faults and won't tolerate for a moment if she discovers he has been discussing her with his friend, his sister or his mother.

Her home reflects her; beautiful, stylish with lovely earth colours and a sense that nurturing is real, the feeling is warm and homely, its sense of timeless permanence fills the deepest need of the home-starved soul. Business-like and efficient in the world of work, she wants her home to be a place where she cuddles up to her soul mate, where they share all the joys of the day and fears for tomorrow. She seeks a mate who understands this and will calm her fears, encourage her dreams and sexually fulfil her.

Parenting is important and she needs to see her soul mate as actively involved in equal parenting. She will nurture his wildest dreams and see them through to a beautiful fruition and expects that he will totally understand when she arrives home from work and says she isn't going to be an office worker any longer but from next month (because she tacks on that she gave in her notice today) a professional artist. She'll play the sensible life game for a while but in the end the needs of her soul grow and flower into an insatiable longing.

Taurus woman is a very good soul and her mate recognises that and loves her for it.

SAGITTARIUS girl stays a girl well into her sixties when she starts to grow up and calm down. She has so many flings and love adventures with such a variety of partners that it is hard to know just what she does want from her love life. Of course, she knows very well; it is unconditional love. It's what she gives, and what she needs. Sagittarius is the sign of no-commitment and many entanglements but she'll keep searching until she finds that soul who will love her as unconditionally as she loves him. When she finds him, and she eventually always does, she feels as though she has come home and never wants to stray again.

As she matures through her teens and into her twenties unbidden, an unusual spirituality grows in her. Her soul begins to make its own demands for spiritual nourishment. Good at denying feelings of sadness and ignoring well-meant messages from her own subconscious, she often blunders off in the wrong direction and searches for spiritual satisfaction in worthy causes (which she drops as quickly as she takes them up) like dog protection groups, left wing political movements, orphanages in India or the protection of some obscure archaeological site no one has ever known or cared about.

She is open, generous and passionate, and yields to physical pleasures, all the while making stern private judgements on a luscious partner who is mean with money, time and emotions. Towards her late twenties and into her early thirties she realises that all the groups thng other than her need for a soul mate. A real soul mate for her isn't driven by anything other than a desire to love, serve and share fully and intimately on every level with a partner ... exclusively, and not with a bunch of people bent on changing the world.

When she understands herself well she knows that her perfect man is to be found in a philosophy class, a walking group, in the local drama group, or a book club. The only party she then wants to throw is a very special dinner for her man. The only conversation outside of work she wants is with him. She will enchant him with her sense of fun, her humour, and win his respect with her clear and very fair assessment of people, situations and possible outcomes of any planned course of action.

Gradually she will reveal the essential goodness of her nature and admire and respect his goodness. He will appreciate that she doesn't try to change him in any way at all, but accepts him totally as he is.

It can all go horribly wrong if she allows her jealousy to make false judgements of his motives or suspect him of affairs or emotional attachments. It's a very rare man who actually enjoys being subjected to a barrister-like grilling about a harmless conversation she spotted him having with a pretty woman. Her honest mind tells her there isn't a scrap of harm in his having a little flirtation in a pub or at a party, that it's actually good and healthy for a man to have male and female friends.

When she does eventually settle she is wise enough to choose a man who cools her fiery nature, then life and love become the haven she has always subconsciously sought.

CANCER girls, when they were little, loved the idea of being grown up girls with their own home and kitchen, beautiful babies to fuss over and love, furniture to polish, a garden in which to grow the lovely fragrant flowers to decorate their home with. Watching her mother prepare and cook the family meals she dreamt of the day when she too would fill her kitchen with all the aromas of good home baking, and watch while her own family devoured her offerings with happy appreciation. She only had a hazy idea of what her husband would look like, knowing only that it would be an early marriage — no living in sin thanks-very-much — and that they would move from the honeymoon into their own nest. But she was always clear in her mind that he would be a good and loving provider. He would be the real man of the world out there fighting battles on the family behalf, earning a living, hunting and gathering and bringing home the necessities to support family life. The home is the altar of life to the Cancerian woman, the parents are the priest and priestess, the children their joint and sacred trust.

Her soul is the mirror of her emotions and will and drive to create the ideal family. Her worship is to family. Her place in the great scheme of the universe is to perpetuate all that is best and nurturing for her family. Socially she can be quite shy and, of all the zodiac, is most likely to have a phobia about going out in public or being shy to the point of silence in a public group. But when her eye lands on a man who is confident, talkative, energetic and with an appetite for and a joy in his work, she glides to him as though drawn by an invisible soul-thread. He becomes aware that she is approving of all he says, laughs at his jokes, is delighted by the idea of his old-fashioned courtesies like offering her a seat, holding a door open for her, giving her a single rose. Without any conscious effort she encourages a man to be a man. She rejoices in his masculinity and expects that he will want to spend some leisure time with other men, on the football pitch or at the golf club. If he is late for a date or uses bad language she will look surprised or a bit distressed so that he won't do that again willingly. Not for the bombastic tactics of nagging or pointing out his faults in public. She would never do that, he is her man, her husband, her mission in life to love him, to please him.

Her soul is a submissive one, she is the feminine complement to his masculinity. If he comes home tired or angry about the events of his day she will drop everything to listen to his account. She nurtures him, makes him well, allows him to sink peacefully into the healthy healing atmosphere of his home. Her home, her altar is a pleasant homely place and she loves the sight of the muddle created, inevitably, by family life. It reassures her.

If he fails what to her are quite normal standards of family life it deeply offends her soul, a dark shadow blots her happiness and she retreats into a silent, hurt mood. If she is usually shy and not greatly into talking about her thoughts and feelings she's hardly going to change overnight, so she retreats into silence, moodiness and sometimes depression. Her husband may call this sulking and wonder what's the big deal about forgetting to let her know that he wouldn't be home for dinner or perhaps forgot to give her a card commemorating their first date. Cancerian woman needs to understand that SHE is the intuitive one in the relationship; that a man of energy and action and speed is not normally a mind reader. She needs to spell out just what it is that bothers her, discuss it with him and move on. Love can't grow, souls don't thrive in a place of brooding, sulky silence.

AQUARIUS woman IS soul. Not the big sad eyes, drooping mouth and wilting shoulders type of soul, but the sort that embraces the entire universe and its people with compassion, grace and inborn understanding. Without even thinking about it (because Aquarian woman is a constant and often very deep thinker) she understands that the soul is the spiritual, immortal part of the person inspiring and guiding the emotions, morals and intellect. She floats above the earthly world seeking other good souls. She is quick to spot a soul-less being and wise enough to know that there are many possible soul mates out there for her. A sexy and fascinating woman, she understands that a man with face and body appeal is not necessarily her soul mate. It is her ability to instantly sum up and KNOW that other person without passing judgement that is her chief appeal. Quite unbound by the earthly values of fair play she homes in on mates who can bond with her, but not necessarily sexually. That's often of secondary importance, it's true friendship she wants. The soul-less she discards in a fraction of a second; for her they don't even exist.

Aquarius woman doesn't reach a particular point in her life when she feels it's time to settle down, get the house, the man, the car, the dog then plan the baby. She is above all that. It doesn't concern her in the least if she goes through fun-filled life with a partner or without because she finds many, many outlets to feed her soul. Her parents, her siblings, her work, her many friends, her interests all feed her delightfully and happily. But when her very aware soul encounters her equal, and she is as interested in his mind and body as he is in hers, she is swift to stake claim. An Aquarian marriage can take place very quickly after the first meeting. She knows within twelve hours if this is the man with whom she can live a lifetime. And, despite caution from family and friends who may consider her their number one eccentric, she is often proved right in her choice.

Their home may not even have a dining table, but it will have a couple of big comfortable armchairs where they'll sit talking enthusiastically for hours on end. Their appetite for each other will be boundless and the bedroom will be an extension of everything else about their lives, unreserved, adventurous and generous. Routine isn't a word the Aquarian and her mate use very much and rarely think about. Mealtimes may be haphazard, holidays spontaneously arranged without much thought or plan, work might be changed at a moment's notice. Interestingly, whilst they talk about the events of the day and the affairs of the world, they rarely sit with a partner and plan life itself. It just seems to occur. If her partner announced that he might take off to Tibet by himself and might be away for three months, she would encourage him, applaud him and send him on his way with her very best wishes. She doesn't give him freedom, for as a true soul, aware, she knows that his freedom is not her gift to him but his right as an individual on his passage through earthly life.

For all her wisdom and knowledge the Aquarius girl retains an endearing naiveté and childlike eagerness for life. She is entirely irrepressible and completely loveable.

It doesn't go wrong for Aquarius woman too often because she chooses wisely. But if she exercises her need for freedom too much, her partner may feel that he is a definite second placer in her life and get uneasy, and demanding of her time and attention. That makes her more aware of her need for individual space and more determined to take it. Aquarian woman has a habit of detaching herself emotionally from her relationship and observing her partner. Unfortunately, she feels the need to share with him her dispassionate observations and can't understand when he reacts with horror or distress. To stop a good relationship from failing she needs to understand that love and commitment are also about compromise and discretion. And she needs to stop delivering pronouncements about his faults and failings as though he were the subject of a laboratory experiment.

Find Your Perfect Love Match
— Avoid That Mistake

———

Ask yourself a few relevant questions before stumbling blindly into a new relationship. Is the man you've fallen for actually free to have a relationship with you? I remember one call from a woman with a pleasant voice. I guessed her age to be in her mid-thirties. She was guarded, hesitantly asking me if she and the man she loved would ever have a life together. I couldn't psychically sense him anywhere near her. I didn't feel that his thoughts or attention were turned towards her very often. As she gave me his date of birth I divined instantly that he was married. She admitted it readily when I asked her but assured me that although he lived with his wife, there was nothing in the marriage, and that he had promised to leave the marriage and set up home with my caller. I felt so sorry for her because the cards showed he would never leave his wife, that their marriage was a reasonably happy one, and that he loved his children to whom he was a good father.

In all my years as a psychic I have met many women who waited in loneliness for their married lover to leave the wife and children. I have never met a man who is prepared to wait patiently and lovingly for his married lover to leave her husband and join him. Men are too realistic.

Of course marriages do end, men and women move on to new and happier relationships. I know that; I've seen it happen many times. All I am saying is that you should check your prospective partner's availability. If a woman is seeing a man once a week, or once every two or three weeks, she is not in a relationship with him. A wife or girlfriend doesn't have to be the barrier; it could be his work, his hobby, his friends. Look at how he spends his time and with whom, because that's where his important relationship lies. If he is in a relationship with you, then he spends a very large part of his out of work time with you.

A woman also needs to check that they want the same things out of life. A young caller was in a relationship with a much older man who had a grown-up family. He had done all the child-rearing and parenting he wanted, and had made it a condition of their future marriage that there must be no children. She wanted to know if he would change his mind as she did want children. The cards showed he would never change his mind. Privately I thought that he was selfish and the love he offered was conditional and not worth very much. He should have chosen a woman of his own age and not one twenty-two years his junior, but I didn't say so. Being psychic doesn't give me the right to make up someone's mind for them, I just say what I see in the cards before me.

Certain signs of the zodiac are compatible, others are incompatible. I do believe that if there is real love it can overcome many personality differences but the following compatibility ratings will give you a guide.

These ratings don't just tell you about your love match, but can explain why you do or don't get on with your boss, or neighbour, or brother or sister.

🐎 **ARIES** and 🐎 **ARIES** — two Arians together are not very good news and not very peaceful either. Aries is a strong, feisty fire sign. One Aries is a handful, the two together are quarrelsome, competitive, and make impossible demands on each other. Aries is quite capable of tolerance, but sometimes terribly intolerant of another Arian. A lot of patience and tolerance would be needed to make this one work.

🐎 **ARIES** and 🐂 **TAURUS** — signs next door to each other in the listing of the zodiac always have difficulty. They don't gel at all. The physical attraction either wanes quickly or only exists on one side. These signs have no intuition about each other, and don't admire the qualities in the other person. A difficult match.

🐎 **ARIES** and 👫 **GEMINI** — this pair really like each other. They are friendly toward each other and can find interest and amusement in each other. Each would regard the other as a real friend. There would be nothing that they could not discuss together. They talk together and perhaps more importantly listen to each other. A very good match.

🐎 **ARIES** and 🦀 **CANCER** — a difficult match. They just don't understand each other at all. They see the natural personality traits in each other as faults and set to work trying to change each other. This relationship will always struggle.

ARIES and **LEO** — a lovely match where each really likes and encourages the other. They bring out the best in each other. Other people look at them and think they are so lucky to have a near perfect relationship and wish for a bit of the magic in their own lives.

ARIES and **VIRGO** — a tough one. There is so little in common that a relationship probably wouldn't get off the ground. Their view of life, of the future, would be so different that it would be like two aliens trying to communicate.

ARIES and **LIBRA** — they just don't understand each other's feelings. The only way this relationship could work is if one party just switches off and agrees totally with the other. Each finds it difficult to see things from the other's point of view. A very challenging relationship.

ARIES and **SCORPIO** — they are prepared for the compromise needed in a successful relationship. They compete with each other and don't give each other credit for anything. Squabbling and competitive qualities emerge that are destructive and unhealthy emotionally. Not a good combination.

🐏 **ARIES** and 🏹 **SAGITTARIUS** — a very good match. They are stylish, funny and intelligent. They approve of each other. They like each other. The best of friends, they are also very supportive of each other. It's nice to be around this combination.

🐏 **ARIES** and 🐐 **CAPRICORN** — these two will bicker a lot, but they do understand each other. Aries won't like Capricorn's devotion to work, but can understand it. Capricorn won't like the way Aries flares up but can see why it happens. They tolerate each other, and for two very different people can actually make a go of the relationship.

🐏 **ARIES** and ♒ **AQUARIUS** — this is a great relationship. They both have a lot of fun in it. They look forward to seeing each other and relate in the friendliest possible way. They also give each other a lot of space, essential to these signs, but they are never far from each other's thoughts.

🐏 **ARIES** and ♓ **PISCES** — signs next door to each other have a lot of problems. This combination spend a lot of time trying, and failing to understand each other. Aries sees Pisces' emotional reactions as weakness. Pisces sees Aries' decisive strength as arrogant bullying. They are very hard on each other.

🐂 **TAURUS** and 🐂 **TAURUS** — they will either bore each other to death or so completely lose their sense of humour that life will be a dull and very hard affair. Not recommended.

TAURUS and GEMINI — they will spend a lot of time scoring points off each other and ridiculing each other without the faintest idea of the hurt they cause. An unpleasant combination to be around.

TAURUS and CANCER — a truly lovely match. These two like each other. It's a wonder they ever get anything done because they are quite happy to sit around all day just talking and listening to each other. There's a happy playful quality to this relationship. This match can last.

TAURUS and LEO — a difficult match. Both signs demand a huge amount of attention and neither are prepared to give much. They can very easily resent each other imagining snubs that aren't there, or sensing a non-existent hostility. Growing apart is not difficult for this couple as there probably wasn't too much togetherness in the first place.

TAURUS and VIRGO — astrologically these two earth signs ought to get on very well together. In reality it can be quite hard for them to get along as they go about things in very different ways. They may both agree on a savings plan, but with entirely opposite ideas on how the saved money should be spent. They press the hostile buttons in each other.

TAURUS and **LIBRA** — not a great match. They can't resist being critical of each other. Taurus believes that Libra is all about image and Libra sees Taurean dedication to work as being a bore. They can't seem to communicate at all.

TAURUS and **SCORPIO** — this is a power struggle with each convinced that their own way of doing things is the only way. They won't give each other an inch. There is usually a powerful physical chemistry between the two which may hold things together for a while.

TAURUS and **SAGITTARIUS** — drive each other mad. They can't ignore each other. They share little and treat each other's differences with a certain amount of contempt. They want to score points off each other. Love and respect can't thrive in such barren emotional soil. When together they are very uncomfortable to be around. The tension in the air is tangible.

TAURUS and **CAPRICORN** — they admire each other. They are deeply appreciative of the other's good qualities. They are loving, supportive and encouraging. They are in tune with each other. This is a happy and very successful combination.

TAURUS and **AQUARIUS** — although they have very different personalities and very different agendas they each make a real effort to see where the other is coming from. They use their best talents to make the relationship work. It's often a case of opposites attracting, but it can and does work and produces a very strong and lively partnership.

TAURUS and **PISCES** — this relationship can be one of the most joyful and happiest. They please each other. The friendship is very strong. They are committed to each other. There is an eternal youthfulness in this combination. Even after years and years together they act, behave and feel as though they are still in the early stages of being in love. A truly awe-inspiring and beautiful combination.

GEMINI and **GEMINI** — this combination can work very well. They will quarrel a lot, but the rows aren't bitter or nasty. They manage to resolve differences while they battle it out. Each will come away from the verbal sparring match knowing and understanding a bit more about the other.

GEMINI and **CANCER** — this one is tough. They can't seem to agree on anything so it's difficult to understand how they ever get anything done. House hunting together will usually end in a row with nothing being decided and no agenda decided on. They can't seem to compromise at all, something they can both do very easily with any other sign.

🜂 **GEMINI** and 🦁 **LEO** — there's a lot of good chemistry between these two. They encourage each other to reveal their secrets and dreams and go on to encourage the fulfilment of those dreams. They want the best for each other. They have a friendly respect for each other. A happy and healthy combination.

🜂 **GEMINI** and 🜍 **VIRGO** — although there are quite a few similarities between these two there are also major differences about how things should be done. They might both want children but have radically different ideas about how the child or children should be brought up. Instead of sitting down and working out common ground and compromise they go head to head in heated argument. When this relationship is good, and it does have its highs, it is very good, but when it's bad, it's awful.

🜂 **GEMINI** and ♎ **LIBRA** — they see only the good in each other. They are a happy and very united combination. They deeply and instinctively understand one another. They talk a lot but in reality much of their communication is spiritual. A great combination.

🜂 **GEMINI** and 🦂 **SCORPIO** — These two are so different that the only way this combination can work is if one party simply switches off and allows the other full rein to dictate all the terms. This is never a partnership in the true sense of the word. If Gemini is allowed the upper hand it turns them into a bully and the true Gemini detests bullies. If Scorpio gets the upper hand it makes Scorpio devious and manipulative, qualities Scorpio hates. Only rarely and with maturity could this relationship prosper.

GEMINI and **SAGITTARIUS** — as long as they give each other a fair bit of freedom this combination can work very well. Gemini appreciates Sagittarius' generosity and open-mindedness. Sagittarius respects the keen Gemini brain and ability to communicate superbly. They fire each others' imagination and each encourages the other's ambition. Together they are likeable and sociable and radiate a pleasure in each other's company that is like a breath of fresh air.

GEMINI and **CAPRICORN** — it's hard to see how this combination can have any commitment to each other since they haven't the remotest idea of what makes the other tick. Each can't understand what makes the other happy or unhappy. Capricorn mistakes Gemini's intensely humane gifts as weakness. Gemini mistakes Capricorn's work ethic as an inability to enjoy life. Not a successful combination.

GEMINI and **AQUARIUS** — this combination is sheer delight to both. They get along easily, effortlessly reflecting each others joy in being alive. They like and respect the sheer goodness they see in each other. They often run into patches when they have no money — this is a generous to family and friends combination — but it only makes their love for each other stronger.

GEMINI and PISCES — this is not a workable combination. They can be outright nasty to each other and then hate themselves for it as neither sign is by nature nasty or spiteful. But Gemini sees Piscean moodiness as self-indulgent and selfish, while Pisces regards Geminian fluency with mistrust and suspicion. They are poles apart and better parted.

CANCER and CANCER — as long as the familiarity they feel for each other doesn't breed contempt this combination can work quite well. Their moods can be frustrating for each of them but they can understand each other's motives. Very importantly they can laugh together, and not at each other. Some other signs find Cancerian moods absurdly childish, but not other Cancerians, they know how and when to take each other seriously.

CANCER and LEO — they can drive each other into a state of rage. They can be verbally abusive of each other and say deeply hurtful things. Cancer rarely sees that behind that Leonine arrogance there is a very vulnerable person. Leo rarely appreciates that underneath that Cancerian moodiness is a highly competent and shrewd brain. They are too far apart emotionally to find comfortable common ground.

CANCER and VIRGO — this most unlikely combination can get on really well together. Cancer can see all the positives in the Virgo character. They make each other feel valued, clever and they usually look good together. In public and private they are intensely loyal to each other, a quality both signs need and respect. They show each other good manners, another quality both signs respect. They are good together.

CANCER and LIBRA — very occasionally Libra can be a cruel sign, and equally occasionally Cancer can be a bully. In combination these draw the negatives out of each other. They actually need a referee to stand by and point out that neither have won the last bout of verbal sparring and both were wrong. They don't listen to each other and on the odd occasion when they do, they don't believe the other. A dangerous combination and not recommended.

CANCER and SCORPIO — Astrologically this ought to work as they are both water signs. In day to day life it turns into a battle for dominance. Neither one is prepared to give an inch. Neither will admit that the other could be driven by motives of unselfish love. To onlookers it seems as though they are bent on not just misunderstanding each other but destroying each other.

CANCER and SAGITTARIUS — this combination can be very kind to each other without ever truly understanding each other. They seem to have an instinctive understanding of each other's needs, hopes and dreams and work hard to fulfil and meet them. Only time will tell if they are successful in their self-appointed task. But they seem to need each other.

CANCER and **CAPRICORN** — there is a lot of mutual admiration in this combination. They each like the qualities they see in the other. If they meet through the workplace they see a lot of good in the other. They like each others families and both respect family values. The physical attraction is the surprise neither expected. It lasts. They work well as a team.

CANCER and **AQUARIUS** — sometimes this match works very well, sometimes it's a complete disaster. Cancer can't understand an Aquarian's complete lack of involvement in the twosome bit. Aquarians can't comprehend the Cancerian need for total commitment. Neither can make sense of the other's emotional needs. Clashes are inevitable.

CANCER and **PISCES** — two beautiful people together making life and love work in perfect harmony is rare and wonderful. Watching these two is like a lovely picture with all the right colours, sounds and aromas of true love and friendship. Cancer and Pisces together represent the good life in all its most natural and rich elements.

LEO and **LEO** — two mad people thrown together can make the most perfect sense of love and life. These two can do it. They can show the world how to fight and win, how to argue and resolve, how to love and be in love. Apart from looking like a couple of movie stars they exude a sort of love grandeur that is awesome. They are a wonderful combination.

LEO and **VIRGO** — neither of them can see what the other is trying to do with their life. They can't see the good in each other, only the faults and flaws. They'll tear away at each other in a horribly destructive way. This is a terrible combination. Detect the bad and destroy the good is their mutual mission. Best kept well apart.

LEO and **LIBRA** — these two can be real friends. They admire each other's physical good looks and like each other's personalities. They like the home life they create together. They both bring out the hardworking qualities in each other, and work together to create a happy and harmonious future. Good match.

LEO and **SCORPIO** — physically this is an almost perfect match. In many other ways these two are capable of creating a superb life together. They want the same things and strive together for it without necessarily understanding each other too well. They are both proud and rejoice in each other's achievements.

LEO and **SAGITTARIUS** — the best of friends, the most loyal of compatriots, the fiercest of lovers, these are an excellent match. They have no illusions about each other, understand each other and believe in each other. One of the best matches in the zodiac. This match can last until the very end of the longest day.

LEO and **CAPRICORN** — they nag each other over the smallest, meanest and pettiest of issues. Most people watching them and listening to them scrapping want to knock their silly heads together. Neither can see the nobility in each other. They don't deserve each other and are better apart — far apart.

LEO and **AQUARIUS** — they could be really good friends. They could go out on the town together, holiday together, encourage each other on to one mad exploit after another. This is a fun combination. Their home would be a wonderful mixture of good taste and a light, free and airy atmosphere. Being around them reminds people that relationships can be a lot of fun no matter what age a person is. Good long term prospects.

LEO and **PISCES** — there would be so many potential minefields in this relationship that it would be difficult to predict who would trip up first. Leo can crush the delicate Piscean temperament with blunt speech. Pisces might wear out the staunch Leo spirit with too many tears. Not worth the emotional effort.

♊ **VIRGO** and ♊ **VIRGO** — they will understand each other and most other signs have a hard time really coming to grips with the fragile Virgoan temperament. They completely respect and agree with the Virgoan anxiety about health, wealth and emotional matters. Others may say that they can't see how two such similar people could make a match of it, but they underestimate the Virgoan capacity for true love and romance.

♊ **VIRGO** and ♎ **LIBRA** — they drive each other so mad that it is impossible to understand how they could ever have come together in the first place. In the unlikely event that they do attempt to make a match of it they soon realise that they have absolutely nothing in common and very sensibly part company. No one is surprised and collective family and friends all give a great sigh of relief that they have stopped tormenting each other.

♊ **VIRGO** and ♏ **SCORPIO** — a great match. These two can be best friends, great lovers and two of the greatest conspirators in the entire zodiac. They like each other, approve of each other and have a rare and complete understanding of the other's personality and motives. Ten out of ten for this match.

♊ **VIRGO** and ♐ **SAGITTARIUS** — they couldn't understand each other in a million years of trying. They like each other, but don't know why. They approve of each other because Sagittarius recognises truth in Virgo and Virgo envies the unconscious freedom in Sagittarius. They each have qualities the other likes and wants. But as partners? Forget it.

♍ VIRGO and 🐐 CAPRICORN — astrologically they are well-matched. They make almost the perfect couple. They like each other, there is a complete understanding that makes poetry of their strong and beautiful relationship. They reassure each other and are completely supportive They instinctively know how to make a relationship work.

♍ VIRGO and ♒ AQUARIUS — they irritate each other. Virgo sees Aquarian freedom as laziness and listens to an Aquarian's skilled and lovely use of language as airy fairy nonsense. Aquarius watches the Virgoan worrying with intolerance; feeling it is nothing but evidence of neurosis, and doesn't hesitate to say so. Not a workable or happy union.

♍ VIRGO and ♓ PISCES — lots of ups and downs with this one. Virgo gets very impatient watching Pisces moon around the place not understanding the mood variations. Pisces thinks Virgo is a nagging nit-picker. If there is true love in this relationship then each would have to make a real and uncritical effort to understand the other. Often a lot of physical chemistry.

♎ **LIBRA** and ♎ **LIBRA** — they like what they see in each other. Each reflects the other's good points. They are proud of each other, recognising that to be always gracious and good humoured requires an effort that the outside world doesn't always see. There is a well-guarded privacy of each other. They are generous and good-natured together. A very likeable combination.

♎ **LIBRA** and ♏ **SCORPIO** — absolutely impossible, a hellish duo, venting spite and sarcasm and sometimes outright cruelty on each other. Each plays the victim to the other's imaginary faults, each plays the role of persecutor with an easy skill. Best kept very far apart.

♎ **LIBRA** and ♐ **SAGITTARIUS** — this is a stunning combination, easy, charming and very good-humoured. There isn't anything they can't talk about. Nothing they won't forgive each other for. They have the same compassionate and generous reaction to life events. They are kind and respectful to each other. This relationship can survive just about any catastrophe.

♎ **LIBRA** and ♑ **CAPRICORN** — there is often a lot of great physical chemistry between these two but they just can't appreciate the strengths in each other. They are also very intolerant of each other's imagined weaknesses. Libra sees Capricorn's drive and energy as dictatorial and Capricorn listens to Libra's attempts to see a problem from every side before reaching a judgement as weak-headed, shilly-shallying. Too many difficulties and not enough joys.

♎ LIBRA and ♒ AQUARIUS — chatty, chummy and charming. They take each other seriously enough so that if the Libran advises the Aquarian to cool down , to the work colleagues face, Aquarius listens and obeys. They are so good to each other and for each other. Great combination.

♎ LIBRA and ♓ PISCES — They grate on each other. In some ways they are similar but they don't like the similarities. They try correcting and changing each other, but they do so tactlessly and can't see when the advice is not wanted or even not necessary. They find it very difficult to tune into the other's moods. This is often a tense, uneasy relationship.

♏ SCORPIO and ♏ SCORPIO — they face a lot of challenges in a relationship. They are mistrustful of each other's motives. They grill each other about what was precisely meant by an unguarded statement. Together they can't seem to lighten or balance the relationship which can sink sometimes into negativity and depression.

♏ SCORPIO and ♐ SAGITTARIUS — this can work, but with some difficulty. These two strong personalities battle it out, each determined to win, each convinced that their own way to do things is the right way. Being a back seat passenger in a car where one is the driver and the other a front seat passenger is a nightmare. They never stop criticising and advising each other. They can't agree on anything. With tolerance and maturity and a real desire to get along together, a relationship can work because they just can't ignore each other.

SCORPIO and **CAPRICORN** — there is a touch of very special magic in this partnership. They are real partners, each one complementing the other. They bring the best out in each other and deliver their very sweetest and best qualities to the table of love. They can work together and live together in a beautiful harmony.

SCORPIO and **AQUARIUS** — the one thing Aquarius values is freedom. This is a free, loving and independent spirit. Scorpio needs to possess, to dominate. Freedom is a threat to Scorpio's sense of emotional security. They will clash over and over again, endlessly repeating their own needs. Neither spends enough time listening to the other. If, however, they can mutually accept each other without trying to change the other then this combination has a chance of succeeding.

SCORPIO and **PISCES** — these two water signs make an awe-inspiring combination. Their whole life together is a journey of love and understanding. If you ever see two eighty year olds together, holding hands and stopping for a long romantic kiss you can bet you're watching a Scorpio and Pisces. They were born to love each other. It is an unselfish love, for each thinks far more of and about the partner than they think of themselves. A match made in heaven.

SAGITTARIUS and **SAGITTARIUS** — when they occasionally cool down after one of their many blazing rows they find in each other truly wonderful gifts and qualities. The rows are over as quickly as they begin and are forgotten and instantly forgiven. They may set out to do some shopping and spontaneously book themselves a bus journey to Poland. What seems crazy to other people makes perfect sense to this eccentric couple. They understand each other very well. They certainly have a lot of fun.

SAGITTARIUS and **CAPRICORN** — a wretched match. They don't even trouble to understand each other. They make their feelings of contempt or boredom quite clear. As each feels more and more loss of self-esteem and depression they can't see that each is incapable of making the other happy. The blame and the recriminations continue until either both or one of them is too weary to continue and go their separate ways. No marks out of ten for this one.

SAGITTARIUS and **AQUARIUS** — best of friends, co-conspirators, allies in everything. They play practical jokes on their friends, throw excellent parties and are at the centre of a large and lively social circle. They take very good care of each other and if anything does happen to upset the balance of the relationship it is immediately tackled and dealt with.

✣ SAGITTARIUS and ✤ PISCES — it's a bit hit and miss, but most of the time this one works. They are both fair and honest and know when they have caused emotional hurt to the other. They are good at saying sorry to each other. The emotion between them is very real and grows in love and respect with every month that passes. They are prepared to work at differences so that they never become irreconcilable.

✤ CAPRICORN and ✤ CAPRICORN — not a great match. They nag each other and forget to reward each other. Also those superb Capricorn manners fail towards each other. Two Capricorns together lose their sense of humour and snarl at each other. They accuse each other unfairly. For instance, if one forgets to pay a bill the other will harp on and on telling the miscreant that it was selfishness or meanness rather than a simple mistake. They are better apart — far apart.

✤ CAPRICORN and ✤ AQUARIUS — this one varies a lot, flirtatious and harmonious one minute, snapping and sharp tempered the next. They arouse a lot of emotion in each other and the relationship is rarely calm. It's certainly never quiet, unless one decides to cold-shoulder the other. It's a case of signs next door to each other not having sufficient empathy with each other. With a bit of maturity it has a chance of working happily, but with loads of tolerance needed.

CAPRICORN and **PISCES** — they are so happy together it's a pleasure to be in their company. They complement each other perfectly, each contributing love and tolerance to the relationship. Capricorn loves Pisces' innocence and truthfulness. Pisces loves and admires Capricorn's sturdy, hard-working spirit. They listen to each other hearing exactly what the other says and means. They bring out a gentleness in each other which is a lesson to anyone witnessing it. A sweet and wonderful combination.

AQUARIUS and **AQUARIUS** — a good, lively mating of kindred spirits. They can be funny, passionate and talkative. The understanding and tolerance is near perfect and the loving respect is total. They never lie to each other, never treat each other to emotional dishonesty. They are tolerant, kind and wise with each other.

AQUARIUS and **PISCES** — very difficult combination. Aquarius simply doesn't understand where Pisces is coming from. Piscean emotion and moods are regarded as some sort of lunacy by Aquarius who keeps hinting that Pisces needs a good therapist. Pisces can't believe or understand that Aquarius is perfectly serious when endlessly analysing friends and life events. Pisces simply thinks that Aquarius is giving vent to thousands of pretentious and unnecessary words. Really can't work.

PISCES and **PISCES** — they poke gently but harmlessly at each other but they truly do understand each other's moods. They also understand the Piscean need for tenderness and deliver magnificently. When this relationship is running smoothly it is superb, they make each other very happy. It can flounder if one spends more money than the other and refuses to change. Neither is materialistic but there is always a need to respect money. If that's not there, there will be quite a few bitter rows.

Recognise Incompatibility And Deal With It

E very Tuesday morning I have a guest slot on television taking viewers' queries. In my radio studio I am alone and it is much easier to focus quickly on my caller. Television is a bit harder. I sit beside one of the show's presenters in front of a camera pointing straight at us. We are watching an item wind up, usually an outside broadcast. As we go into a commercial break a couple of large very bright lights come on illuminating our set. Someone hands me a list of callers on stand-by. I scan the list quickly before handing it back. The floor manager takes a quick check that our microphones are live and well hidden — clipped at the back of the waist band. A red light flashes on above the camera, the floor manager raises a hand to let us know we are about to go live. I blot out the figures moving quietly about the studio floor as the presenter reads the introduction to my slot from the auto-cue on screen. Our first caller is greeted.

'I want to know if my relationship has a future.'

As Mary from Clare is speaking I am shuffling the oversized deck of cards I use for television and trying to get a picture of her in my mind. Her voice is brisk, too controlled and I get a sense of a woman trying desperately to hold her emotions in check. I look at the cards and see that although the marriage is in serious difficulties and that her husband has already left home, there is a spark of hope for a happy and united future. I am dealing with a couple who are very different but not incompatible.

They want the same things from life, she is a Capricorn, he is a Taurean, astrologically they are compatible. But as very often happens in this match they have focused on the financial and practical side of the relationship and neglected the emotional and physical needs of each other. I also sense physically that they have been through a long and stressful period during which life overwhelmed them. It's hard to feel tender, loving and understanding when you fall into bed every night fatigued with the events of another very hard day. But for Mary and her husband spending time talking, listening and finding a way back into love is not impossible.

Incompatibility is quite different. The two people want completely different things from life, there might be impatience on one side, indifference on the other. The physical spark that first ignited the relationship died very quickly and when it went they found that there was no friendship, no respect, no liking for each other. If one has a stronger personality than the other, then it may hold them together for a little while. They don't watch the same things on television, like the same holidays, handle the children the same way, eventually they don't even listen to each other. Different signs handle incompatibility differently. Some make it easy, others make it very hard.

PISCES woman ignores all the warning signs once he has said those three magic words 'I love you'. On the basis of that statement she instantly commits herself to him and plans their rosy and romantic future. She overlooks the fact, while she furnishes their dream kitchen in their future home, he hasn't held down a job for longer than three months since she's known him. She believes that he will stop spending all his leisure time with that group of friends she knows are bad for him. She really believes that going to live with his mother is only a temporary measure. He may not even want to go public on an announcement that they are actually a couple. But she can explain that one away too. It's not that he doesn't love her, it's because he treasures the privacy of their romance and anyway, doesn't secrecy add a bit of spice to love?

If he puts her down in public she reasons that he is insecure and it's actually a sign that he needs her all the more. She works harder to reassure him, love him and keep the dream future alive. It's worth it because he had told her that he loves her and she believes him. It's hard on her to endure that lonely fortnight when he went on holiday with his friends and didn't phone or text her, but she is happy if he is happy. Her own life is filled with love for him, her job, her many friends — why shouldn't he be entitled to as much fun as she is having? The fact that she is unhappy and often lonely in the relationship is only slowly acknowledged by her.

The other sort of man she attracts and is attracted to is the serial clinger. In the early days of the relationship it was wonderful proof of his profound need for her.

When he told her his whole happiness depended on her it was an aphrodisiac. Gradually even she, the ever-loving sign of the zodiac, becomes worn down with his constant need of her company, his ceaseless need to be told that he is all and everything to her.

She may resign herself to her fate. Some Pisceans are very good at the resignation. If a child or children are in the equation she may put up with him for their sake. But gradually she begins listening to family and friends because she has confided in them early on that all is not well. Not that she really needs to because she has an expressive face and eyes and all her feelings are mirrored there. Many people love Pisceans and are quick to see the signs of neglected love, unhappiness and incompatibility being endured.

If she hasn't resigned herself to the misery of an incompatible relationship she will start fighting with him, pointing out his failures and telling him how unhappy he is making her. Resentment against his friends grows. Anger at sexual rejection turns her into an unhappy nagger.

Pisces woman finds it incredibly hard to let go, to acknowledge that the romance died and the rosy future only existed in her head and that her chosen mate was never capable of delivering her dreams. Usually it is her mate who will do the leaving, but even then she clings on to the hope that he will return and that he really did mean it when he said, 'I love you'.

GEMINI woman doesn't see the glaring incompatibilities in her relationship. It's often the differences that attracted her in the first place. It is her duty in the relationship to put him right on quite a few things. She has a strong moral sense and an innate knowledge of what has to be done to make a relationship work; especially where a child or children are involved. Having analysed the faults in her head in a practical and realistic way she points out to him how to be a better father, a better provider, what her needs of him are and what he has to do about it. The logical and practical outcome of a relationship in which two people love each other and live together means that everything is shared fifty-fifty. The money, the housework, and child-rearing is mutual. If he has lied he must own up, and promise not to do it again.

Gemini is often an unconventional sign in terms of career, place to live, friends and entertainment but she is from a conventional background and in a relationship her expectations are conventional. It's all about living together rather than loving together. She won't take the words, 'I love you', as his permission to treat her with anything other than the fairest of treatments. If he can't earn a whole lot of money she deals with that and budgets with whatever she has and usually does very well, but she expects that to be acknowledged. After all if it's a partnership that's going to work she expects praise and recognition for her efforts. Failure on his part to see things her way is notched up and will be pointed out at frequent intervals.

She isn't too concerned or critical about what he does for a living and will encourage him to realise his full potential. His full potential has been decided by her quite early on. She explains it to him and points him in what she conceives to be the right direction. If he falters or tries to evade her she pushes him sternly back on course.

Incompatibility is a word or concept rarely used or recognised by her; she knows that she can mould him into what she wants him to be so long as he does what she tells him to do. She shares all her own hopes and ideas with him and expects his full backing for that course she is taking up, that business she wants to start up. If he advises her that her business plan needs modification she doesn't listen because she sees this as evidence of his negativity, not his superior judgement. If she points out the flaws in his friends she expects him to drop them and takes it as a sign of his disloyalty if he continues on in the friendship.

Gemini woman simply doesn't recognise that she is living in an incompatible relationship and tries harder to get him to change. She pounces on counselling and urges him to go to get better. Breaking up is not an option. With all his faults she is committed to him and will work ceaselessly to bring about the improvements she knows are best. She accepts unhappiness, failure and arguments as part of her lot once she has committed. If he dares to speak of his own unhappiness in the relationship, or criticises her in any way at all she is angry and outraged at his treachery and demands to know who put him up to it.

Very occasionally, for Gemini woman is fundamentally loyal and faithful, she will cope with an incompatible relationship by having an affair. It props her up, helps her feel good about herself and helps her cope with the unsatisfactory partner she has come to despise.

No one is surprised when they part company except Gemini woman. She is deeply and profoundly shocked and hurt. 'After all I've done for you', she'll say, bewildered as a little girl. After the first savagery of her anger abates she is left with abiding bitterness, sometimes for years, until she moves on and meets a new love.

♍ **VIRGO** is unlikely to get into an incompatible relationship because she has thought about it during the early stages of the relationship. She recognises it very quickly and uses her emotional intelligence to visualise the unhappiness that must be the inevitable outcome of two incompatible people trying to live together, raise children together and relate as a couple to their families and friends. She knows what she offers in a relationship and what she needs. She will recognise if a man has the qualities she needs and values, and will part from him quickly and without resenting him if he doesn't match up to what she knows she wants. Even if she's pregnant by him, she will prefer single motherhood with his part-time support to the hell of incompatibility. She is very realistic and can taste and see the nightmare that can only result in two completely unalike people slowly strangling each other emotionally. She has the foresight to understand that love and respect and friendship can only grow in conditions of compatibility. She understands totally that compatibility means mutual tolerance and a sense of compassion for each other.

If she quite accidentally strays into an incompatible relationship she will exit definitely and very fairly. Only if she is deeply religious and her convictions prevent her from moving on with the speed she needs, will she stay in such a relationship. It's not if, it's when. She'll take into account the religious convictions I've mentioned, the state of the mortgage and the ages of the children, but she simply could not live with incompatibility. Her head rules her heart and she can operate whilst still married by moving into another bedroom and organising her life so that her partner is definitely an ex, albeit an ex she can turn into a friend. She will be just and businesslike about the break and her head won't be swayed by pleas to change her mind or stay in a relationship where she can't co-operate on every level with her partner. She is honest and her honesty compels her to set her partner free and seek freedom for herself. She is well capable of moving on, not necessarily to another relationship, simply moving on to an emotionally freer space.

Her ex will find her a good friend, even a good companion and certainly scrupulously fair in any financial, legal, property or child issues. She will even go to his wedding if he marries, or marries again as the case may be. She will be genuinely happy for him if he finds a compatible partner with whom he can be happy. She is relieved not to turn into a frustrated and worried nit-picker and re-builds her life looking for satisfactions in quiet order and harmonious family life.

If her ex comes back and wants to try again because mutual love may still remain she'll think about it, but probably won't be moved to change her mind. She values her peace very much.

🦁 **ARIES** just doesn't get it about incompatibility. If you love the partner you have chosen you get on with it. Aries woman's judgement is usually fairly sound. It's something she's proud of. This is a very proud sign. Any sort of failure is something taken directly to heart and knocks Aries confidence hard. She also likes to be in control of her life. Finances are handled well. Her job runs smoothly. The sexual side of the partnership is always stimulating and unreserved. They have a lot of real fun times together. She works hard and plays hard. If house renovations, repairs or decorations are needed she works at his side. Holidays are jointly chosen and always enjoyed. So what is all this talk about incompatibility? What can be done about it? She is a doer of deeds, a mover in the game of life. It's all about action. If there's a problem she focuses on the solution. Because she is so much a creature of action rather than thought then the next bit is difficult for her. It's not that she's incapable of rational thought, she is, but her thought processes are so rapid and conclusions reached so quickly that she scarcely notices them.

Her first reaction to his statement that he wants out of the relationship is one of disbelief. Then anger; blind and blazing anger. It is subdued when she watches him wearily packing a bag. He backs away from her awkwardly mumbling something about talking about things later. In the absolute silence following his departure she begins slowly to acknowledge that the 'things' he wants to talk about are the disposal of their earthly possessions. The house, the car, the furniture, the dog. If there are children it will be about who gets to see the children and when. It probably won't enter her mind that access or custody would come into this equation. She may have misjudged his mating compatibility but not his parenting skills. In that terrible moment when her whole life is reduced to a page in an account ledger of who gets what and when, she begins the agonising process of looking into herself.

Emotionally naked and defenceless before a dreaded fate this proud and fiery woman will weep and plead with the distress of an abandoned child. Her confidence vanishes into darkness with the swiftness of a tropical sun. Humbled before the very life she blazed through with fire, passion and pure joy she begins the long painful road to recovery. And recover she will. She will seek the counselling she secretly despised others for seeking. Every positive attempt is made to understand herself, him, life, the past, the Universe. Aries woman in aftershock begins a journey of thoughtful discovery that will alter the pattern of her life.

She learns by degrees (sometimes literally as a lot of Aries women go off and get some sort of qualification after a break-up) that she is capable of all sorts of things, all sorts of pleasures, that life offers her many riches emotionally.

Aries woman doesn't run helter-skelter into a rebound relationship. She might not have a relationship again for a very long time. But next time around she knows what she is looking for. Once her relationship is over, she accepts it's over. She moves on.

She can turn rejection and failure into a magnificent triumph because she understands what went wrong and why, and learn from her mistakes.

TAURUS woman sometimes confuses compatibility with what each partner wants out of life in material terms. If they each want a stylish wooden kitchen with terracotta floor tiles overlooking a walled herb garden, that's compatibility. If they effortlessly agree that they want their children educated in a school with small class sizes and plenty of access to music and art, that's compatibility. If the savings plan includes decent life assurance, good medical coverage and a pension to ensure growing old together in a content and stress free time, that's compatibility. The bit about mutual tolerance of each other's differences somehow escaped her.

Differences frighten her. She doesn't see them as a chance to allow mutual growth or understanding but as something that threatens her relationship and are to be discouraged. If he has a taste for music that is alien to her she struggles to understand him so that he can be swayed away from things that make her feel uneasy. The very thing she most fears — that they will grow apart — happens before her eyes and she cannot see that it happens because of her own intolerance. She only sees that she has set standards, that they are right and that anything different is a direct threat to her happiness and a defiance of her as a person.

Her reaction is one of fear, that is hidden behind a dictatorial attitude. This attitude drives him further into following his own pursuits, inclinations and friends. Unable to understand what is happening and unwilling to sit and discuss it and HEAR what he is saying to her, she retreats into tight-lipped silence. That disapproving silence is the breeding ground for the disintegration of whatever remained of the relationship.

Fiercely proud, she is determined to protect her property and children and would rather go it alone than woo him back. Their incompatibility is further evidence of his failure as a partner and parent. Her heart is breaking, she doesn't know how to talk to him and watches with heartache as each day reveals him, in her eyes, to turn into a stranger. Even when she moves into another room and cries herself to sleep each night from grief and loneliness, her brain is planning another trip to the solicitor to wind up the partnership firmly and finally.

Poor Taurus woman is rarely equipped to deal with incompatibility. It was something that happened to other people. With hindsight it may occur to her that they were two very different people from the outset and that sooner or later change would have to occur. Once she has to doubt her own judgement it could take a very long time for her to regain her self-confidence. Eventually she will be once again the happy, confident woman planning a future with a man she loves and respects but it may take her a very long time.

It can really only happen successfully when she sees for herself what role she played in the break-up and that it was never a matter of whose fault it was but an inevitable outcome of two incompatible people trying to live together.

✿ **AQUARIUS** woman chooses her partner with such delicately tuned intuition that she isn't very likely to settle for someone with whom she is incompatible. She has some sort of built-in mechanism in her brain that steers her quickly and sharply away from any sort of incompatibility. However Aquarius is one of the most complex signs of the zodiac. Other signs share a set of characteristics that make them quite recognisable. But there are as many types of Aquarian as there are signs of the zodiac. One type of Aquarian recognises that they are the wild one of the zodiac so they look to the experience of friends and relatives. Ah, that's what settled them down, getting the job they wanted, spending a good few years travelling or getting married, or moving in with a partner. They borrow from other peoples' experiences. If it worked for them it'll work for me, they reason. So they get into a relationship when they have reached a stage in their lives where they want to change from being a free-wheeler into a stable member of society.

A relationship is only the vehicle they have chosen to achieve this end. It's like the equivalent of taking an antibiotic to cure an illness. Take the medicine and it will work. Being a very strong personality they are likely to attract an equally strong personality. These two strong personalities move in together and expect life to work out. But the Aquarian was chosen for her very strong personality, her quick wits, her readiness to talk, laugh and sometimes act just a little bit stranger than everyone else.

When her new partner discovers that overnight she seems to have changed into a woman who wants a mortgage, cocoa at eleven, and is hunting through insurance policies for the most suitable life assurance plan, he feels that he has made some sort of horrible mistake. She forgot to tell him of her plan. When, and if, she does tell him he feels he has been the victim of a plot and then the trouble is out in the open. They started from very different emotional places but end up in the same one — getting out of the relationship as quickly as they got into it.

The other sort of Aquarian whose relationship is bound to end because of incompatibility is the one who is attracted to someone they can laugh with a lot. They think: this is good, I like this, I'd like a lot more of it. The Aquarian woman falls effortlessly into this relationship and for a while loves it. Gradually her partner is expressing other needs and wants, which she calls demands. She has not understood that along with the readiness to laugh, to treat life as a big joke laid on to entertain her, her partner had the need to be loved, to be understood, to have his highest ideals expressed and expect encouragement of his ambitions. She sits back and analyses him freely, sometimes cruelly, and always with an emotional detachment from any pain her behaviour may cause.

The incompatibilities are treated as a joke until the game bores her and she moves on. He is out of sight and out of mind. He may be read as an interesting chapter in her history. More than likely not. She knows how to move on and stay gone.

CANCER woman understands her relationship through her feelings. Only when it is all over is she capable of analysing it and seeing that they were incompatible. Even when their incompatibilities jump right up at her she doesn't see them for what they are. Sometimes the weekend she had looked forward to doesn't happen. In her mind she had planned that they would go shopping together, choose a present for her mother's birthday, visit his sister and the new baby. Maybe they talked about going off to somewhere idyllic and having a romantic weekend together. Somewhere in the country, romantic, hidden away, a candle-lit dinner and an old-world room in a hotel. Come the Saturday morning and he is loading golf-clubs into the boot cheerily telling her he is off with the lads for a weekend of golf and what is she doing on Tuesday as there is no sport on the television. She won't say anything, it's not her way, she hates scenes, rows, confrontations. So off she goes to buy the presents, do some shopping, visit that sister all the time carrying the mobile in case he rings her. He is never out of her thoughts and can't believe that after all they shared she is out of his thoughts. On Saturday night she curls up with some chocolates, a box of paper tissues and a weepy and romantic movie, the phone nearby in case he calls. By eleven she is worried in case the reason he hasn't called is because he has had an accident.

She can't sleep because she is worrying that maybe she should ring around the accident and emergency departments or the gardai. Then it comes home to her that he didn't actually tell her where he and the lads were going. When he eventually surfaces she hides her feelings and murmurs something about hoping he enjoyed his weekend. If he tells her it was fine but gives absolutely no other information she doesn't question him. When he tells her that next weekend he is all hers and that they will go to the best and biggest shopping centre of her choice, she is thrilled. He wants a new laptop and some more sports gear. She feels privileged to be so important and a necessary part of his life. If he's vague about when they next have a date — because he is so swamped with work — she understands and is never far from the phone in case he calls.

Her brain doesn't function until too late to inform her that she chose him because he was a strong, masculine man, a lad amongst lads and that caused her a secret pride to have captured him. That such a man is a million miles away from understanding doesn't occur to her. Also, because of her dislike of confrontation she hasn't actually spelled out her own needs or her distress about not having them met. It comes as a sort of blinding to the recognition that they are incompatible. The realisation does come, because Cancerian woman is no emotional fool. She endures in unhappy but ever hopeful silence until he disappears from her life completely. Even then she still goes on hoping. New relationships are all measured against all that was best in that incompatible one. She feels hurt and disillusionment but that is outweighed by all the times he made her feel happy, secure and loved. Even when hope dies, her love never quite dies.

🦁 LEO woman often has a first and very serious relationship which may end in them living together or marrying. It usually starts young and lasts a few years. Her mind and body and emotions are all in tune and she knows the very moment when she became aware that they were growing apart. She is also aware that her partner knows very little of her feelings at this stage and believes that they are happy together and goes on talking about their future. She agrees half-heartedly to all the plans he is busy making. In her mind she is gradually but surely detaching from him. Bit by bit she gets impatient with him and begins to despise his renewed efforts to please her. Even when they go out together to buy that lovely and expensive sofa he saw her touching and admiring she is fantasising in her head about that man she works with, or the one she met in the supermarket the other day. She may not actually have secret affairs but she does begin by thinking all the time about other relationships.

Fundamentally she is a very honourable person and may not in the early stages think that a permanent parting is the solution. But every day brings her closer to realising that they are incompatible and that the situation is unbearable. If he asks her if anything is wrong she is likely to snap at him, making him cautious about asking again. She rings up all the old friends she dumped when she got fixated with him, or fell in love with him, or became infatuated with him. Seeing old girl friends and going on girls' nights out are her political right, she tells him. He can't stop her anyway. She might change her job or suddenly decide to resume a broken education. Whenever he tries to talk to her about their growing differences, she tells him that he is clingy, possessive and that she is only acting like a grown-up member of society.

Gradually life with a man she feels she has nothing in common with becomes absolutely unbearable and whether or not there is another man there, she will leave. Usually she allows a discussion about her relationship with her partner to turn into a full scale row and she marches out. But not there and then, only when she has had a good night's sleep and found herself another flat if they are living together.

She allows the apparent anger she expresses to keep him at a distance while she sorts herself out. But however much he pleads, she won't go back. She feels a sense of relief that the relationship is over. If she had been suffering recurring headaches and they suddenly disappear, she knows she was right to leave a relationship that no longer fulfilled her. Her natural decency may lead her, unfortunately, to be totally and devastatingly honest with him. It's too late, of course, for him to do anything about it.

If it is he who leaves her and she has had no idea that he feels that they are incompatible she reacts with anger, hurt and a ferocious unwillingness to give in or accept that he no longer wants what she offers. If her red hot emotions were a spear he would be dead and gone. If he leaves her for another woman she makes WAR. After a long time her innate honesty tells her the break-up was good and has freed her to start all over again.

♎ **LIBRA** woman is a curious creature. She operates always on two levels. The surface level rejoices in her partnership. He looks good, has a good job and in public they are an attractive and gracious couple with lots of friends and in great social demand. In private he is attentive to her many needs and demands. They share tastes about décor, food and fashion. It all looks good and appears almost perfect. On her second level she is by no means the romantic she appears. It would be difficult to find anyone more realistic, shrewd and calculating than Libra woman. She is acute and intuitive and saw very quickly his faults and imperfections. She knew perfectly well that he didn't get that promotion he was after because he wasn't smart enough. That money he was supposed to pay that garage bill with didn't get mysteriously lost; he gambled it. He wasn't working late that evening he didn't show up, he had escaped from her and went on a drinking spree with his friends.

She has such a need to be part of a twosome and an equally strong need to display this in public in all its perfections that she balances her need against his inadequacies and pretends to look the other way. But her need and craving for constant displays of love and reassurance keeps rearing its head and won't go away. Her emotions keep getting in the way of the perfect picture she wants them both to figure in. Anxiety about abandonment is never far from the surface of her life. When he creeps off to do his own thing she feels rejected. Like a desperate child she begins checking up on him, phoning his workplace, ringing around the bars he may be in. She might phone his mother with tearful complaints, tell his best friend that she is being badly treated, or worse, try to make friends with his ex to compare notes.

He reacts with anger, keeps an emotional distance, gets even more secretive until he drives her as mad as she has driven him. Her pleadings with him to change, to understand her, to address her unhappiness, fall on deaf ears. 'If you really loved me, you wouldn't treat me this way,' is her constant cry of reproach. 'What do you want me to do?' he yells back. 'What I tell you!' she screams in genuine agony.

She wants to go out on public and elegant displays with him, but she also wants just the two of them curled up in front of the television. Love that is incompatible is still love in her eyes and should continue on. This tough, realistic woman can be surprisingly child-like and naïve about the nature of real love. Gradually her unhappiness and lack of fulfilment wear her down. She stops checking on him, tracking his movements, confronting him about his lies and failures. What she doesn't accept is the possibility that her behaviour ever had anything to do with his reactions.

Temporarily she'll hate him, but she begins the next campaign of courtship a much wiser woman. She moves on, finds another partner and starts all over again rebuilding her life and working towards a happier future. All heart and all brain is this ultimately sensible and warm-hearted woman.

SCORPIO is quick to see where the incompatibilities lie. Scorpio woman is normally intuitive and decisive in action. Deeply romantic and essentially loyal, she will weigh each factor against another. She may have rushed impetuously into her relationship but she won't exit either swiftly or easily. If the relationship is in the early stages she may end it and move to another partner with a bit of regret but she won't entirely forget. If the relationship has got to the stage where she feels that maybe six out of ten of her needs are satisfied then she'll wait it out. Attractive looks and a satisfying physical relationship are very important to her, but there are other things that count. If her partner is well-off and powerful she is drawn to this combination of qualities like a magnet. She likes these qualities and will overlook quite a few incompatibilities if his wealth and powerful position are guaranteed to last. For a while she will try to mould herself to be what he wants. Scorpio lady is highly adaptable; she is a survivor, she understands the process she has to go through to turn potential failure into a triumph.

If he is argumentative, critical and negative she'll practise teasing and tempting him out of bad moods. At first she pretends to agree with him, then actually begins to see life through his eyes. If he is a persuasive talker she will come to believe that she may actually be wrong about everything and that his criticisms of her are justified. She begins to act passively in his presence. After a while, although she continues acting in the way he wants her to act, she begins to hate him, even dread him. What all this does to her self-esteem is obvious, it sinks lower and lower. But it also gives her permission to have affairs. Although essentially a sensual and sexual woman, her true nature is intensely loyal and faithful.

A dreadful downward spiral of conflict in the relationship, conflict within herself and often a depression, make her incapable of action. The parting comes if he moves out or she meets someone else who gives her the self-confidence to leave the destructive relationship. Even when they formally part, separate, divorce, one part still thinks of him as her real partner, especially if there are children. She will go on hoping that they can be friends, and she works on that. What she really wants, still, is his approval. It could take a long time and a lot of support from the new partner before she accepts that she doesn't need the approval of an abusive and incompatible ex to live a happy and content life.

SAGITTARIUS woman had all the exit routes checked out before she went on that first date. She didn't think too deeply about the next six weeks, let alone the next six months. Unlike other signs who wondered on the first date if he was the one and only for her and hoped it would last a lifetime, she never gave it a thought. If he ever hinted at such a possibility she would have run to the nearest exit. But if the relationship was easy and friendly her mind might turn to the idea that spending Christmas with him would be a fun idea.

Then she would think of all the other people she would like to have around at Christmas and that twosome might turn into a meeting of family. As soon as family accept him as her partner she begins to think seriously about them as a couple. Real love may be there, real commitment, but she still wants her freedom to go off with her friends for the weekend, or the week, at little notice, and may make her plans without any reference to him. If he objects, she will be genuinely surprised and may even ask what business it is of his. If she gets a phone call from an old boyfriend who wants to come and stay the weekend she can't see what her partner is making a fuss about when he objects to the visit. Miss Sagittarius simply cannot see that her partner might see the relationship they have in a different light, might have different expectations and might actually be right. She is quick to express her irritation at the restrictions he puts on her. She can't bear to be limited, controlled, curbed.

The very freedom she needs as her life blood is often the major incompatibility in their relationship. Whilst freely expressing her opinions about his relatives, she fails to explain that she actually likes them and all this free-wheeling talk is only a game for her. He has to spell out his hurt with big gestures, tears, even threats to leave before she begins to take him seriously. At this point she will sit down and really think hard about the relationship. A major drawback for Sagittarian women is the denial or suppression of feelings of sadness. Because all the while she is thinking and talking she is checking out the exit signs. Her mind leaps ahead to have a look at how she will live alone.

It may take her a long time to admit that she is in love and maybe longer to accept that compromise is just and necessary. She isn't the soldiering-on-in-dogged-silence type. If she feels that he is her best friend, and truly loves him, she will try to make the adaptation, to accept their differences peaceably and live happily ever after. If she concludes it can't be done, she'll rationalise it all, explain it all, make all the businesslike arrangements for parting and express the hope that they can still be firm friends. And she really means it. No one is better at moving on and keeping ex's as friends than Miss Sagittarius.

🐐 **CAPRICORN** woman will keep a firm eye on the bank balance. Very often she and her partner have gone into business together. Equally often she discovers she is better at business than he is. Increasingly she makes all the business decisions with only a token discussion with him. They have a very good life style, beautiful furniture and a holiday home that was a very sound investment. If she had to think for a moment of the effect of all this on the balance of their emotional relationship, of how he might be feeling, she would never understand it or see it in a negative light. Making money makes sense. She despises other women who have the philosophy that the car is always his and the kitchen is always hers. The idea that money making might be sometimes sacrificed if their emotional relationship is to succeed would be a madness she could never agree to.

If there are children and they are doing well at school and have hobbies and nice friends she congratulates herself, and him sometimes, on their success as parents of a future generation of good and upright citizens. She is incapable of thinking outside herself to see just what sort of role model she is presenting to them. They may observe her drive and energy with approval and learn to despise their father. All the emotional conflicts that this brings into the home may be outside her emotional imagination. If there is any sort of disruption to the smooth running of the home she is confused and puzzled. That she may be the cause of it never enters her head. If she is accused of it, she is deeply wounded. It was never the way she intended life to be.

She believes that work is the great salvation of mankind. If her partner is lazy and won't work, she despises him. If he spends recklessly or gets into debt she tackles him head on and calls a halt. Briskly she sorts the problem out but demands, quite rightly, his promise that it will absolutely never happen again. If he reneges, it's all over. Living with a man she cannot respect is the emotional death that will kill all the love she ever felt for him. It kills the future she knows they could have together. She always looks forward to peace and prosperity in the future. If he can't share that view and desire it, she can't live with him.

Capricorn woman isn't very good at telling her man that she loves him, she prefers to show it in all sorts of practical ways. If he is ill she will be his nurse and friend. If his business fails, or he loses his job, she's right there at his side helping him to get going again. But if he can't appreciate this she knows in her head that they are better apart. They want different things from life and are better off to live it separately.

When all the finalities have been completed and the signatures dry on the forms and documents that signify the ending of the relationship, she goes home to her empty house and climbs alone into her expensive and comfortable bed. She begins to think about what relationships really mean. The quietness disturbs her. She wants his key to turn in the front door lock. She longs suddenly to have him there beside her as she reaches over to touch the empty space. She remembers all the times he reached for her but she was too tired, too worn out after another busy day to respond to his need of her. She cries herself to sleep wondering what if things had been different.

Recognise The Love Rat

—◆—

In this chapter I am going to show you, by using a few simple manoeuvres with a deck of ordinary playing cards, how to spot:

- If your relationship is for keeps
- If your relationship has a happy future
- If your man is cheating on you
- If your relationship can survive his affair
- If your relationship is over

In my thirty-year career as a successful psychic I have been struck over and over again by the depth and insight of womens' intuition. With little to go on they have a sharp and distinct feeling that something is wrong in their relationship. The not knowing is the worst part. If he is having problems at work, has money worries, or has an addiction, most women feel at the outset that they can cope, help in some way. What the woman dreads is the intrusion of another woman into the relationship. That is the big dread. It might spell the end of the relationship. She has to confront herself and ask if she wants the relationship to go on. Most do.

It is often true that the man is last to know or even suspect that his partner has been cheating. Men are very trusting — unless they have always been jealous and suspicious, but that is something quite different. Women have an instinct about the affair almost from the moment it starts.

From the moment a woman's suspicions are aroused she begins to watch her man, quietly, without him noticing. She notes that he is spending longer in the bathroom, that he has joined a gym, that he has started going to get his hair cut or styled on a regular basis. He may start taking sun-bed sessions. When she gets out the holiday brochures he may warn her in advance that he has a lot of work to do and that she may have to go alone. His mobile phone is often switched off. He comes home late. He goes off for golfing weekends with his friends. She searches his pockets looking for evidence. Whenever she can she checks his mobile phone. Sometimes she rings him at work. I have had clients amongst those I see for psychic readings in my office who will hire a private detective to put their man under surveillance to gather evidence. This is the sort of woman who will gather her evidence before making an accusation.

The other type of woman will blurt out her fears and suspicions in an angry outburst. She watches his reaction to test the truth of her fears and suspicions.

Most women desperately want to be proved wrong. Neither type want to admit that the man they love physically and emotionally prefers another woman. It is the greatest and deepest hurt. They also have a similar reaction when the partner swears that there is no affair, that there are a thousand reasonable explanations for the behaviour. That she is mad to even think such a thing and should find a therapist to help her get better. They waver, back down, even apologise to their man for thinking such awful things about him. His denials are a secret relief because it means that he doesn't want his marriage or permanent relationship ended.

Of course, if he admits it and says that he does want the regular partnership over then she is truly shattered and may begin to plead with him to stay, to abandon the other woman.

Once a woman suspects that her man is cheating it has got to be brought out into the open, discussed and find out if there is a way forward. But the cards can show you if there is or is, not a happy future ahead.

CARD MAGIC

Take an ordinary deck of playing cards and remove the two Jokers and all the Twos, Threes, Fours, Fives and Sixes. Put them to one side. You will not need to use them again. You now have thirty-two cards remaining. Shuffle them very well. As you are shuffling the cards, wish that the relationship you are in has a happy future. You can do this if you are in a long-term relationship or you have just started a relationship. (But not if you just wish you were in a relationship with someone you find attractive). When you have given the cards a good shuffle, put the deck face down on the table and with your left hand cut the deck once from the top and lay down the top half by the side of the bottom half. Now two piles of cards are on the table in front of you. Turn over the left-hand pile so that the face of the bottom card shows. Then turn over the second pile so that the face of the bottom card shows. If the Nine of Hearts is on the top of either pile, then you can be certain that your love affair or relationship is for keeps. No matter what has been going on, your relationship is going to last. If the Seven of Hearts appears beside the Nine of Hearts you have true and lasting love.

If the Ace of Spades and the Eight of Spades appear on top of the two piles of cards, your relationship has no future at all.

If neither of these combinations, or cards, appear on top of either pile, take the right hand pile of cards and look through them. Ignore the left hand pile for the moment. If the Ace and Eight of Spades appear one after the other, this is bad news for the relationship. If the Ace and Eight of Spades appear on either side of a King card then this mean that your partner does not really want the relationship to last. If the Seven of Hearts and Nine of Hearts appear together ,or on either side of a King or Jack card, then your man loves you and will stay with you.

If two black Eights appear on top of the two piles you have cut, it means that he is cheating. It may only be a temporary infidelity; he may come back to you. You need to check the outcome of the affair before taking any action. Two black Eights together, or on either side of the King or Jack card also mean infidelity. To find out something about the woman with whom your partner is being unfaithful, you need to lay both piles of cards out in a row. Do it first with the pile of cards on the right, then with the pile on the left.

Beside the black Eights will appear a Queen card. If it is the Queen of Diamonds, then your man is having an affair with a woman with light blue or grey eyes and blonde or sandy hair—it could be either natural or dyed. How she appears in public determines her colouring, not her colouring underneath the hair colouring. If the Queen of Hearts appears, then the woman has light brown, auburn, chestnut or mousy coloured hair. The Queen of Clubs shows a woman with dark blue or dark grey eyes, fair skin and dark hair. A woman with very dark eyes and very dark hair is the Queen of Spades.

Remember that infidelity does not always mean the relationship is over. Any man may commit an infidelity and still love his partner and not want to leave her. He thinks of his affair as something on the side of his life, not his future.

The love rat makes a habit of infidelity. He takes all the good that his wife or partner offers him in terms of domestic stability, a good home, care of his children, and him when he is ill, him when he is broke, or loses his job — but has no intention of giving up his affairs. He is a permanent cheat.

The two black Tens appearing either together, or on either side of the King or Queen card, mean quarrels, sometimes very bitter words, and it forewarn the card reader to beware of saying things without meaning them.

The Seven and Eight of Hearts appearing together means that your man is a flirt, but he is probably only interested in you. They are a nice combination of cards to draw because they are telling you that your man is honest and friendly, likes women, but wouldn't cheat on you.

Now gather up the deck of 32 cards and shuffle them again, this time thinking of you and your partner and wishing for happiness between you. Lay them all face down on the table in a long line. Take any six cards and turn them over and lay them in a line before you. If a King and Queen are in the line up it shows you as a couple. If only the King shows in the six cards, it probably means that he thinks more of the relationship than you do. If only the Queen shows it means that, at the moment of reading the cards, the woman values the relationship more.

Don't worry if a King or Queen does not appear in your six-card line-up. The six cards still have something valuable to say about your relationship. Ideally, a dream line-up would contain the Seven of Hearts and Nine of Hearts, the Ten of Diamonds, the Ten of Hearts and a King and Queen. That would be just perfect, a loving and socially attractive match. The Seven and Nine of Hearts, as I've already explained, means true love. The two red Tens can mean happy and loving surprises. In the six-card love cut they mean that the physical side of the relationship is a very happy one.

Almost as good is a six card line up where the two red Eights, the Eight of Hearts and the Eight of Diamonds, either the Ace of Diamonds or the Ace of Hearts, and the Ten of Hearts and Jack of Hearts show. This foretells a wedding. The Eight of Hearts and Eight of Diamonds are the wedding cards. If the Ten of Clubs appears, it indicates that you will most likely consider marrying abroad.

If you don't get the combination of cards you want to see, don't keep shuffling and cutting the cards as that defeats the whole purpose of the exercise! The first reading is the most accurate one. Even if you are disappointed with the information the cards are giving you, it is as important to know when a relationship is not going anywhere, as it is to know if it is going to succeed.

As you will know, there are four suits in each deck of cards: Spades, Diamonds, Clubs and Hearts. Each of these can signify something different for you.

The Spades are not particularly good omens. They are negative cards. The Ace and Eight of Spades together mean the outright failure of a relationship. The Seven and Eight of Spades together mean that your relationship causes as much depression as happiness and would need really careful assessment to decide if it is worth the trouble of continuing with it. The Eight and Ten of Spades side by side predict heartaches for you. It might only be temporary, but it is a very real check if you had hoped to be with your partner for ever. If the Seven and Eight of Spades appear on either side of the King or Jack card, then it shows that your man is suffering from either anxiety or depression. His behaviour might have changed and you might have suspected that he has a love interest elsewhere. The Seven and Eight of Spades are telling you that this is not so. He may be worried about his work, or even your relationship. The Seven and Nine of Spades together mean an absence of love. Again, this might only be temporary. If, for instance, the Nine of Hearts appeared in your six card line-up then you can take heart because it means that somehow your relationship will survive the difficulties. If you are unlucky enough to draw all Spades in your six card selection from the thirty two cards, it is showing that your relationship is undergoing really severe difficulties and is unlikely to survive them. But this would be a very rare selection.

Diamonds are about communication. The Seven and Nine of Diamonds either side by side or on either side of the King or a Jack are telling you that your man is not a very good communicator. Perhaps he never tells you that he loves you. That's because he can't communicate, not because he does not love you. The Eight and Nine of Diamonds usually indicate someone who is secretive and hates giving away information. The Nine and Ten of Diamonds together show someone who absolutely detests being questioned about anything. They feel invaded if asked questions. It is a combination of cards often shown in a line-up when enquiring about teenagers. Teens often go through a phase when they become secretive about their activities outside the home. It's a normal and very natural phase in their development, which most parents recognise and cope with. It's only harmful in an adult relationship when one party is either mystified by their partner's silence or feels excluded outright from their partner's life.

But remember the Diamond cards showing are really helpful because their presence indicate that your partner is not deliberately ignoring, hurting or excluding you. He simply never mastered the essential art of communication.

The Club suit is about money and business. These are, what I have always thought of as, the lively cards. They show lots of activity around a person, or a person who is mentally and physically very active. If you are cutting the cards to find out about a new man in your life, and they show two or three Club cards around the King or Jack, then you have met a man who is ambitious, a hard worker and provider. The Ten of Clubs is the card of travel but, cut beside a King or Jack, it foretells that the new man in your life is most likely a foreigner. A lot of Club cards in your six card line-up can also show you a man who is a bit of a workaholic. You might have to accept that you come second to his work. If you know that you are an emotionally needy person who depends solely on your relationship for companionship and support, you might find yourself quite lonely with such a man. The Eight and Nine of Clubs are always a very successful combination relating to the world of work and money, but also reveal that your man is conscious of status. If he didn't get that promotion or lost his job he would be hit very hard and would take it so seriously that his ability to function in the relationship, or to his friends or children, would be seriously affected.

The Seven and Eight of Clubs drawn in the relationship cut show a man who might conduct every conversation with you as though he were engaged in a business meeting. It also shows you that he probes and looks for answers to just about every aspect of your life together. He would want to know exactly how you spent your day, how much everything costs, what plans you have for next week, next year or even the rest of our life. You might even feel as though he were a barrister cross-examining a witness in the court room. It isn't a bad sign, it's just the way his mind works. He is curious about everything and he likes being informed. If you select the Seven, Eight and Nine of Clubs together then you aren't getting the most romantic man in the world. He won't be whispering too many sweet nothings in your ear. On the other hand, he will never tell you a lie. He is direct and truthful, and he'll demand the same from you. He probably won't hold your hand too often, but he'll certainly hold his promise to care for you, support you and defend you as a most sacred trust.

I've mentioned the Ten of Clubs as a card denoting travel, or even a man from overseas, but cut beside your man, it can also mean someone is very restless and always wanting change. While this can be exciting at first, it can also lead to an emotional state of uncertainty. It may be telling you that your man will never be quite satisfied with anything and is either always on the move, or always wanting to change things. A man like this can be hard work.

The Heart suit is by far the best suit if you are looking for love or wanting to find out if your man is truly loving. All Hearts in your six card line-up shows a man who is all heart and soul. He might even be governed entirely by his heart. In a love relationship this is not a bad thing at all. He is a loving man, a tactile man who shows his feelings easily and can talk the language of love effortlessly. He relates openly to everyone around him. The Seven and Eight of Hearts show a man who is a flirt — he might flirt with all your friends, and even your mother. He is a charmer, a seducer of the iciest woman. He is irresistible — and he knows it. The Hearts show a person who is truly good and kind and wants to share joy and friendship with everyone around them. Heart cards around the King or Jack show a man who has never lost the child-like capacity to believe in that bit of magic that turns a dull, grey world into a place of brightness, hope and beautiful colour. He will overcome problems easily because he will always focus on the solution rather than the problem. He will always look optimistically towards tomorrow. If he looks at a heavy grey skyline he will search for the little patch of blue. He is wonderful to go on holiday with, he knows how to enjoy himself and he will throw himself into the spirit of every occasion. He will plan Christmas with you and enjoy it every bit as much as an excited six year old.

If you are sad about something, even bereaved, he will share all your feelings with you and you'll find in him the best friend you need to talk to and love you through bad times.

The Nine of Hearts is the best card in the entire pack. It is the wish card. It shines like a beacon of hope and success. No matter how bad things are, or how impossible they seem, if you cut the Nine of Hearts you are guaranteed success. If, for instance, you separate and are left heartbroken, the Nine of Hearts tells you that your relationship will be back on again at some point.

The Heart suit is the one of love and promises true happiness for you. This suit also shows you that your man is sincere in his love for you; three or four Hearts in your six card line-up show you that he might be a charmer, he probably will flirt outrageously with every female from five to ninety-five, but he will love you and only you for the rest of his life. If you are in doubt about the relationship, or even think it's all too good to be true, three or four Hearts together are telling you that you need have no doubts or fears about his fidelity or love. He is yours, if you want him, for keeps.

Do not worry if none of these cards or combinations of cards are revealed in your own reading. This may be down to the timing being wrong. For instance, if you have just started a new relationship and are unsure what you want from it or how you feel about the other person, you may not be able to find out how he feels about you, or if your relationship is going to last, simply because you are not sure if you want it to last just yet. If you wait a while and try again you will find that your circumstances will be better suited to finding the answers you seek.

Another reason why the cards may not come up with answers may be that you are asking the wrong question. For instance, if you want to know if your relationship is likely to last and be a success, but are actually only hoping to get into a relationship with someone you admire or find attractive, you will not find out if the relationship has a chance of succeeding if that relationship has not yet begun, or if this man you like doesn't even know you find him attractive. Ask a different question — one that definitely refers to your present situation and circumstances — and you will find answers.

Dumping That Love Disaster

Throughout my long psychic career I have often wondered why certain women stay with a man who is no good, does not love them and does absolutely nothing to make them feel loved or valued. A woman will phone into the radio or television show to tell me that her husband drinks, or gambles, is never at home or doesn't give her enough money to keep food on the table; maybe even is physically violent towards her, yet she wants to know if there is a happy future for them together. I list out all the negatives she has given me and can't resist asking what exactly it is she finds so loveable about him. When she tells me that despite all the horrors of her life with him, she still loves him, I wonder to myself what her notion of love really is.

If a woman wants change in her life she must start with herself rather than try to change her man. This is not something most women want to hear. They wonder if I, as a psychic, can somehow come up with the magic wand and show them how to bring about change without actually having to do anything about it. The practical answer is that I can't. What I have learned from my listeners and from my clients who I see on one-to-one sessions in my office, is that different signs of the zodiac react to failure in their relationships quite differently.

Some signs of the zodiac can see quite clearly that the relationship they are in is failing, is going nowhere and that the man they are in love with can never deliver what they need and want. Others live in the vain hope that something will happen to bring out love, or a return to the love they once shared. But knowing that she lives in a failed relationship doesn't necessarily mean that a woman will walk away from it.

I can understand the practical reason why a woman will stay with an unloving man — the house they jointly own, the children they have together, the family ties that bind them, the fact that they have put in twenty or thirty years together and it's just plain easier to grow old with the devil you know. But sooner or later, unless he moves out and on with his own life, a woman in a failed relationship has to make a decision about her own future happiness. If she can't or won't take action to dump her love disaster she must at least ask herself why on earth she is continuing to put up with it.

✎ SAGITTARIUS woman finds it quite easy to move on. If the relationship is in the very early stages, she takes note of things like lateness for a date, broken promises, lies or gross differences between them. She reads her man's character very quickly and doesn't fool herself about his ability to change. After a few dates she calls a halt to the relationship and moves on, maybe with a bit of regret, especially if he was physically attractive. Sagittarius woman is very good at separating the fact that she finds a man physically attractive from her knowledge that he is no good as a person. If he is mean with money or very selfish this registers with her very clearly and very early on in the relationship and she won't consider a future with such a man. It might suit her to be seen around with a man other women want, but her mind is made up, she won't play him for keeps under any circumstances. She notes too, things like sexist or racist attitudes — they deeply offend her. Smutty jokes don't amuse her. All these things are telling her about his mind, his character. She won't share her life with a man who offends her principles or her idea of fairness or decency. Her self-esteem is high and she is quite capable of living happily alone.

If their relationship is of longer standing, or if they live together, whether or not they have children together, she will try to adapt to changes in the relationship. If he has an affair, she will demand that he end it and promise that it will never happen again. But it will eat away at her and she will bring it up each and every time they have a difference of opinion. Her common sense will tell her that they can't live that way. She must either put it behind her and shut up about it, or part company and start again. Sagittarius woman simply can't bear being unhappy. She can survive financial hardship, unemployment, his inability to deal with money, and would most likely take over the role of financial management herself. But she can't live with a man who disrespect her either privately or publicly. She can't live with a man who neither respects nor esteems her. She is a physical woman but can't and won't tolerate mental abuse or physical violence. His first slap will be his last.

If he won't move out of the home then she will. She will give him the chance to change and be supportive of him if she makes sincere attempts to mend his ways, but there is a deadline in her mind. She is entirely realistic about him. Even when she loves him most dearly, she sees the sort of faults and failings that make true love impossible. She is realistic in what she can expect of him and what she is prepared to give in return. Parting will be done in sorrow, but with finality. Once she has made her decision to move out and on there's no question of a second chance or reconciliation. Once it is over it is completely over. They both know where they stand. They may salvage a friendship. She will certainly bear him no grudge afterwards and may even wish him well in his new relationship, but she spends a lot of her adult life trying to recognise and avoid disaster. She thrives on happiness and success and is lucky enough to have been born with that knowledge.

CANCERIAN woman lives in the hope that something will happen to change her love disaster into the fine man she needs to make her dreams of blissful love into reality. She makes endless excuses for him. It was his upbringing, his previously failed relationship, his sensitivity, his anything at all rather than the reality that she loves a man who is no good. Because she herself is naturally good and wants a normal relationship that will lead to a secure and loving future she expects that he thinks and needs in exactly the same way. She can't see that perhaps he is a bully. In her eyes, he is asserting his masculinity. If he is an alcoholic she prefers to believe that it is a temporary phase he is going through and all will be well next week, or month, or year. Once she loves him and believes that he loves her, it is only a matter of time before he emerges in what she thinks of as the real him, the him behind the unsatisfactory facade. The real him, the man she thinks she knows is really nice, kind and loving. He told her that the reason he verbally abused her or threatened to strike her was because she drove him to it, and this causes her to mend her ways and try even harder not to provoke him. If he spends his leisure time sprawled across the sofa watching television it is because he has had a hard day and deserves to rest. She explains away his lack of attention to her by saying that she knows that, deep down, he really loves her. She is tolerant to the point of martyrdom. Cancerian woman has a sort of religious zeal about martyrdom, pain and suffering. Entirely feminine herself, she has a notion that men, real men, are tough, freedom loving and intolerant. Even if her own male role models — her father, her brothers — are kind, quiet and decent, she has a sort of Heathcliff complex and believes that real, one hundred percent, rugged he-men are not far off a great ape.

The more the relationship is falling apart, the harder she searches for the goodness she is convinced is lying just beneath the surface. She is passive and accepting of the most atrocious man and willingly goes on serving him with an endurance worthy of sainthood. Even the children, her very lifeblood and reason for living, are sometimes forced into adapting to his moods or bad behaviour. If he is intolerant of their noise, she drills them into being quiet. If their toys lying around annoy him, she sweeps them out of sight. If he is rude to her friends or relatives, she stops them coming to the house.

Cancerian woman suffers in silence, rarely looking for help or support from anyone. She tries to maintain her dignity in the face of bad treatment from the one she loves. She adapts so much to emotionally unhealthy circumstances that she often becomes physically ill or depressed. She may, but only may, attempt to change herself if she sees that the children are suffering or are being damaged. She is attracted to a controlling man, but if she sees that his control over the lives of her children is so strict that they are being harmed, she may try to limit the damage.

It will sometimes take either an outsider, or some terrible domestic catastrophe to make her see that she has become addicted to his bad behaviour. It may take her a long time to accept that there is no good in the man she loves, that she does not need to live with unhappiness and that she even deserves love and respect. Before giving in and admitting that her love is a complete disaster she may go to relationship counselling, trying to find or revive that good in him, that romance she still feels exists somewhere.

She is incapable of dumping him and can not see a way forward for herself if she leaves him. She will go on loving and trying. She may spend, or waste her whole life with a man who does not care for her and has no intention of ever changing. Eventually he may run out of steam and they dwindle into old age. She his devoted servant, he the cantankerous old wretch he has always been. Being together is what counts for her. Reneging on her marriage vows is flying in the face of God. Only rarely could Cancerian woman take such drastic action.

🐏 **ARIES** woman hates to admit defeat in anything. But she won't put up with a man who doesn't fulfil her either in bed or emotionally. She attracts all sorts of men, because she is usually physically and emotionally fiery and attractive. But the attraction must be a two-way affair. She has no firm conventional ideas about how a real man ought to act, she only knows if he doesn't match up to what she wants and needs he gets his marching orders. It is done swiftly and with a minimum of words. She will know after the first date if he is for her. When he asks her for a second date she simply says it's not happening, she doesn't spare his feelings. She wasn't put on earth to put up with losers. She understands herself very well, knows her needs and limitations. This self-knowledge is her greatest asset and protection in all her relationships. She expects to be treated by him the way she treats him. If he criticises her cooking, she will make an assessment as to whether his criticism is fair and justified. If she thinks his judgement a fair one, she will change and do things his way. But if she thinks he is being unfair then she tells him.

Things don't build up and fester in her mind. Each issue is dealt with and discussed as it arises. She would probably not have chosen a man radically different from her. It's the similarities that attracted her in the first place, not the differences. Always in her mind was the picture of her man. He never had to be perfect, she is too realistic to believe in perfection, but always had to be the sort of man she instinctively understood. She has to like and respect his value system. She wouldn't waste a moment on a man she could not respect. It is a fatal love mistake for a man not to respect the Aries woman. She values her good points very much and won't tolerate a man who doesn't equally value them.

Inevitably relationships change with time and if Aries woman realises a few years into the relationship that she and her partner are going in different directions, or that he has changed drastically, she will take stock, then talk to him, listen to what he has to say and make a decision about whether or not to leave him. Although she is quick and feisty about most things, she won't dump him unless she feels he is a hopeless case. If he is a disaster she will dump him efficiently and without pity and she won't come out of the partnership without very adequate recompense. When it is over, it is over and she moves on, not necessarily to another partner, but certainly to a very content life alone. In quite a short space of time she will regard him simply as someone she once knew and doesn't particularly like any more. She won't hanker to get the relationship back and won't dwell on what might have been. She accepts things exactly as they are, without blame or recrimination, and gets on with her life.

TAURUS woman often attracts a man in love with her physical beauty, who is incapable of meeting her many and deep emotional needs. She can be a fairly quarrelsome woman at the best of times. Sometimes her debate is stimulating, sometimes funny, and often insightful, and more often than not it becomes quite heated. Because she is used to him she doesn't always see that the debates ending in quarrels are becoming the way the relationship is conducted. That she is living in a disastrous and destructive relationship is apparent to everyone except her. I have seen Taurean women go into complete denial about the nature of the man they claim to love. She may claim to thrive on quarrels, believing that in trading insults, lines of communication are open and the relationship healthy. She clings on to what she has, unwilling to give anything away, even her disastrous partner.

Very often she doesn't mean the terrible things she says in a fit of anger and believes that he doesn't either. Truth becomes blurred. He tells her he doesn't love her, that he has had affairs, has spent all the money they jointly earned, and she thinks he is saying it, not because it is true, but to hurt her feelings. When she has calmed down, she resumes life as usual, thinking normality has returned. Quick to spot the dysfunction in the relationships of others, she often doesn't see what is under her own nose.

In a funny sort of way Taurean woman becomes dependent on her disastrous partner. She contributes to his madness by goading him on to even worse behaviour. If he gambles, and she is often attracted to a gambler, she will fling down money defiantly, telling him to gamble that. Remember that old expression about cutting the nose off to spite the face? — that's Taurean woman all over.

Taurean woman flounders on in a disastrous relationship because she does not know how and when to call a halt to it. Change is always painful to her. She will endure the madness of the disaster zone because it is familiar territory, and familiar territory is preferable to the unknown that separation might bring.

She can't and won't dump him; he'll have to do the leaving. When that happens she lurches on, alone and embittered. It may be over, but in her mind he is still her partner. It takes a long time for the peace and quiet to get through to her, to reassure her. She wakes up one morning a long time after it has ended and realises she is content and that contentment was never her lot in her disastrous partnership.

♎ LIBRA woman is likely to make a disastrous match if she pairs off too young. In her teens she just wants to be with someone, anyone. She hates being alone. But she often judges unwisely in her first mate. It never worked from day one, but she wouldn't admit it. She's one of the signs most likely to attract an abusive partner. Her self-esteem is often very low and she secretly believes that somehow she either deserves her wretched lot, or can't do any better. Although she makes some attempts to fight back she quickly adapts and becomes passive in a disastrous love affair. I can think of three or four Libran women clients who hold down very good jobs, have plenty of friends and bring up their children as best they possibly can, yet they continue to live with abusive partners. What they call their relationship, or marriage is nothing but one round of abuse after another. From verbal abuse through infidelity to physical abuse, they hang in there. Librans generally have huge difficulties in making up their minds about anything. They absolutely hate having to make a decision, and find it torturous to make the decision to leave the relationship. They are almost a natural victim of a man who has shown his bullying qualities from early on in the relationship.

Librans hate being alone, hate being single, and a bad, disastrous relationship is still that — a relationship. Any relationship, they reason, is better than being alone. They fear loneliness more than they fear and detest the man they live with. They weigh up the insanity of the relationship against the possibility of loneliness and they stay put. Gradually they lose faith in the future and take each day as it comes, hoping it won't be as bad as yesterday. It always is, and is always getting worse. Even when the distance between them has opened so wide that they may as well be living on different continents, Libra lady stays because she likes to talk about herself as being part of a couple.

If the separation comes, it won't be of her making. She will rarely summon up the courage to dump him. When he dumps her, she will fall once more into the victim role. In her mind it is never, ever really over.

SCORPIO woman endures a bad, mad relationship and in some ways even gets some enjoyment from its wilder elements. She is very good at focusing on what is good in her man and excusing what is bad. She prides herself on her ability to forgive and forget. She can carry these qualities to silly extremes. Her attachment is very, very deep and can survive full-scale war in her partnership. Differences attract her at the outset, they amuse her, intrigue her, keep her guessing. If he stays out all night on a drinking binge, she just waits for him to sober up in the morning. If he leaves the party early with another woman, she waits for him to beg forgiveness. If he never remembers her birthday or the date of their first anniversary she forgets it too in time. If he ridicules her in public she is hurt but won't show it. In her quiet way she brushes it aside, as if it is of no importance. If he tells lies she acts as though she believes him. Beneath her apparent facade of acceptance, is a terror that he will leave her, and she cannot deal with the trauma of having all her habits thrown into disarray. What changes things for her is meeting someone else who treats her well. This is a surprise for her. Bad treatment in her relationship never made her fight back, it caused her to lower her expectations of life itself and feel unworthy. Being well treated, falling in love again, gives her something to measure her bad relationship against. It will take her a long time to dump her love disaster, but when she does do it, the deed is done, with finality. She won't go back, won't try again. He can make any promises he likes, it won't shake or alter her in any way.

Once free of the headache of her awful relationship, she'll wonder why she put up with it for so long and marvel at what she endured.

Of all the signs of the zodiac she is most likely to dump a man who will never forget her, always mourn her loss and work very hard to win her back. But she won't go back into the prison of a bad relationship, once she has left. She is very, very good at learning from her mistakes.

VIRGO woman is practical and sentimental all at once. It would be unlikely that she would get herself into a disastrous relationship. She is good at looking ahead and foreseeing the outcome of an ill-matched pair slugging it out emotionally. It's not for her. Neither does she have any illusions that he'll change. She knows that fundamentally people don't change. They may be capable of changing some habits, but not the fundamental personality. Even on the first few dates her mind is running a checklist. If he is obviously a disaster zone, she probably wouldn't go out with him in the first place. If it becomes clear to her early on in the relationship that things can't work out happily between them, she simply allows the relationship to fizzle out without saying anything. But if they move in together and the relationship takes a turn for the worse she will talk to him, listen to him, try for a compromise, maybe get some relationship counselling and measure the improvements. If improvements don't happen and happen quickly she announces that the relationship is off and she'll take quick but businesslike steps to put an end to an unhappy state of affairs. Virgo woman never expected every day to be a happy day. She is a realist and knows that some points of disagreement must arise.

But it doesn't mean that these disagreements actually have to be disagreeable. Money is often an issue with her — how it's made and how it's spent. Stupidity over money causes her to lose respect for her partner, no matter how much she loves him. Sex is another major issue. There are times when she needs a huge amount of physical attention and other fairly long periods when she prefers to live in loving celibacy. If these sorts of differences can be resolved with goodwill she won't be anxious to change. If they can't she gets more and more unhappy. Unhappiness is unhealthy and she won't endure it. She is a very straightforward lady who deals with life in a simple and effective way.

She dumps her love disaster as a matter of necessity and moves on gracefully. Too dignified to badmouth him, she will simply let her friends and family know that they are parting company and probably won't give any details. Respecting her own privacy, she extends that to him. The two can often remain friends after the parting.

♊ GEMINI woman is attracted to hopelessly dysfunctional men. She often treats his quirks with a good deal of humour in the early stages of the relationship and she often gets a huge kick out of his bouts of emotional lunacy. She hates being bored. When it's quite obvious to everyone else that her love affair is a complete and utter disaster she continues on quite happily, oblivious to the fact that her emotional needs aren't being met, that he is completely unreliable, is probably not as quick and intelligent as she is, and that he has early on in the relationship become completely dependent on her. She sees his clinging as love. She likes being the thinker and doer in the relationship. Gemini woman has so much going on in her life that she doesn't quite notice what is going on in her relationship. Her love needs are met by a huge circle of friends. Her ambitions are met in her own job or career and as long as he debates with her she believes that the relationship is working. Marriage isn't too important to her and a lot of Geminis I know as friends and clients have been quite happy to live with the partner. Always unconventional, Gemini often fails to see the differences between herself and her partner are nothing to do with them being an unconventional couple and all to do with them being completely mismatched. At first she will be wounded by his coldness. She hates a lack of response; can't handle it at all. Sometimes she can't bring any insights to bear on why he is behaving as he is. All she knows is that she is hurt by it. If he refuses to eat the food she has cooked — she prides herself on her great cooking skills — she is angry, accusing him of being childish. She can't see that he is playing games with her, maybe getting back at her for being brighter, smarter, more motivated than he is. Essentially she is above board and never plays mind games, and can't see when he is playing games with her. All she knows is what she is feeling. She struggles to get back to the point when they were madly in love and couldn't bear to be apart. Gemini woman doesn't give too much thought to the future. She is very much a here-and-now person and has effortlessly mastered the art of living in the present.

If she feels prolonged unhappiness in her relationship she will then look to and think about the future. It often depresses her if she is in a disastrous relationship. But she is a realist and can deal with it.

Typically, at this stage, Gemini woman turns to something to console her. It might be comfort eating, it might be taking on a new and much more demanding job, it may be changing her image and spending a small fortune on clothes or the hairdressers. All these activities are delaying tactics. She knows the break-up is inevitable. If she decides to do the dumping she'll do it with kindness and consideration. Everything will be out in the open, discussed, with reasons given. She'll even give him support if he needs it. If he sorts himself out, she may well give the relationship another try. She can be very forgiving and humane. If there is no hope of a reconciliation she will certainly wish him well in his new life while she gets on very happily with her own.

🦁 LEO woman detests being unhappy. It makes her physically sick. If something is wrong in her relationship she will work fast and furious to put it right. If it's not fixable she quickly admits that to herself and takes steps to wrap up the partnership neatly and finally. A relationship usually starts up because of his irresistible physical attraction. Even if she discounts him as a potential life partner, she is quite happy to be with him for as long as he physically attracts her. Uncommitted emotionally, she is at her best — great fun to be with, a fabulous and ready sense of humour, a wonderful talker and always looking sensual and well-dressed.

Although she likes spending most of her free time with him she keeps her own friends and interests and demands little of him other than all the husky sweet-nothings and physical passion that make her happy. But he is falling in love, drawn like a moth to her bright Leonine flame. When he asks her to marry him she is surprised but accepts. A lot of Leo women have a first and failed marriage or serious relationship. She drifts into it without giving too much thought to the future. Before long the relationship ends in failure and she simply can't bear it.

Without giving it too much thought she blurts out her feelings. There is little in the way of guile in the Leo woman. She says exactly what is on her mind at the precise moment the thought enters her head. Once it's out in the open — that she wants to leave — she goes about the business of dividing up the possessions and putting the house on the market. He might be falling apart emotionally, begging, pleading with her to change her mind. He might be baffled, with no idea that there was anything wrong. She thinks he must be emotionally dense not to see that their relationship has become unrewarding, stale, and that there are irreconcilable differences. She acts without pity or mercy. It is not a matter of emotional outpouring, it is quite simply putting an end to a situation that no longer attracts her.

Already she is planning her next encounter. She may have a new partner lined up or she may be planning a hunting expedition. Leo woman at any age is attractive to men, both physically and emotionally. She knows this and moves out of the bad relationship and into the sunshine of her future with perfect ease and confidence.

PISCES woman often attracts relationships that just can't work. Starting out with the best intentions, she often ends up in a love scenario that is like a very bad play: badly scripted and badly acted, with unlikely endings. Like a child she blunders into the love disaster zone again and again. She believes in her man. Once she believes in him and loves him she invests him with all sorts of qualities that she wants him to have. That they aren't there and will never in a thousand years be there is something she won't acknowledge. The smallest and simplest things make her wildly happy. He might have ignored her for three weeks, then turn up with a bunch of red roses and all is forgotten and forgiven. He might use bad language, which she hates. Pisces lady is very much a quality person, and she pretends not to hear. She hates smutty jokes but when he makes them, she pretends to find them amusing even if she doesn't quite understand what he means. He may not turn up for a meal she has spent a long time preparing and cooking, yet she quietly and even without resentment puts everything away and doesn't embarrass him by mentioning the non-event.

She accepts his explanation about seeing his ex and staying overnight at her place because she is still distraught about the break-up, at face value. It's not that she is passive or a victim in a bad or disastrous relationship, she is just plain accepting. Hating others for interfering in her life, she won't say anything to him because she would consider that interference. As I have already said, the Piscean is very much a lady. She has a quality of refinement and good principles about her. Yet time and again she accepts bad behaviour in her man that she would never dream of handing out to him.

It is only with real difficulty that she can she get out of a bad relationship. Her reluctance to exit has to do with her belief in him. With absolutely nothing to go on and a ton of evidence to the contrary she believes in his goodness and his love for her. She never demands proof of his love, just accepts that it's there. It's not. Everyone around her could tell her that. But she smiles less and less, doesn't laugh much and finds herself crying for no reason she can think of. Her tears and depression are over everything and anything except for her relationship. She clings on, even when he moves out or stops phoning or texting her. I've known Piscean women to wait days and nights by the phone, waiting for that call to tell her that the relationship is back on. Sometimes months later she is still waiting in hope; hope that he will change, hope that he still loves her as much as she still loves him.

CAPRICORN woman gets into a bad relationship for all the right reasons. Right, that is, to her. He looks good, sounds good and is a terrific worker. If he is likely to be a controller she sees him as a man who is well disciplined. When he is being rude and overbearing she calls it being direct and straight to the point. Not paying his way she sees as him being quite rightfully careful with money. If he is emotionally cold in public, she interprets that as his being socially correct. She often attracts a fussy, critical nit-picker who can be possessive and jealous to an extreme degree. In the early stages of the relationship she is flattered by his jealousy and possessiveness, seeing it as a sign that he loves her and only her. As the relationship unfolds she comes to see his qualities as a sickness and withdraws from him. She won't give him up though. Capricorns have addictive personalities. Once he becomes her addiction, she is obsessed with him. However overbearing, even cruel he becomes, she stays at his side, taking everything he throws at her. Unfortunately the more he vents his inadequacy on her, the more her own true feelings open up. She gets in touch with buried feelings of love, hate, anxiety, tenderness. They are all muddled up together. Her mind tells her that the relationship is pure madness but she doesn't know how to get out of it. Her pride will often keep her there. Also her unwillingness to admit that she has made a mistake keeps her there. Capricorn women are ferociously proud and independent and only seek professional help with the greatest reluctance. Normally they don't confide in their family members what they are going through or feeling. Keeping up appearances is very important to them.

Capricorn woman often needs a lot of counselling to open her eyes to the true nature of her disastrous relationship. Even then, getting out of it is painful. It reveals all the insecurities and vulnerabilities she didn't realise she had. Once it is over it takes her a long time to recover and often makes her unwilling to enter into a second relationship.

Once peace is back in her life she can step back and look at the relationship for what it was and is often horrified by what she allowed to happen to her. She often feels a degree of guilt, accepting that her co-operation was needed to allow her partner to treat her so badly.

🐎 **AQUARIUS** woman jogs along happy in a nutty relationship. It keeps her interested in the beginning at any rate. But if it amused her at first that he broke all the china on the kitchen floor in a rage, it stops being funny when there are no cups to drink from or plates to eat off. His screaming abuse at other motorists might make her smile in the first heady days of their romance, but she won't smile for long when she realises that his rages are not confined to other motorists, taxi-drivers, lorry drivers, bus drivers and women, but can erupt at her, her family and her friends. If he slams out of the house in the morning because his egg wasn't boiled the way he likes it, she will lose her ability to shrug it off and greet him on his return home with a hug and a warm smile. Aquarius woman sometimes attracts men with rage, or men with addictive driven personalities. The moment they feel unhappy in the relationship or understand that the man they have invested time and trouble in is incapable of rational thought, the relationship is over.

Aquarius woman is extremely liberal, tolerant and unconventional, but she won't take nonsense from anyone. The love she gives is unconditional. She is one of the most delightful free spirits of the zodiac. She is definitely not one of the martyrs or victims. Her place is at his side as his equal. She won't take second place to his addictions. If he can't talk to her about his problems and focus on a solution then she quite literally has no time for him. He is not functioning as a human being. If she can't count on him as her best friend they are finished. She informs him and moves on with speed and deliberation. Their affair is over. If he contacts her when it is all over and they have gone their separate ways she is surprised. Curiosity might tempt her into seeing him again, but she wouldn't re-start the relationship. This one learns from her mistakes and has no intention of repeating them.

Handling Children Effectively

———◆———

The ⚡ **CAPRICORN** child is delightful, very warm and close to his or her mother. Your Capricorn child will watch you and copy and want to do everything you do. He or she will also want to stay physically close to you. If you are in the kitchen doing the washing up then your Capricorn little one is very close on your heels and probably trying to drag a chair across to the sink to join you, helping you. That's what Capricorn children love doing, helping out. Get your little Capricorn a miniature sweeping brush and dustpan and watch them go, all business, across the kitchen floor. They watch carefully as you cook and as early as possible like to get involved. Give them a bowl and fork and let them mash potatoes for you. It might go all over the place at first, but you'll be surprised at how quickly they master this task. I think that's probably why Capricorns turn into such good cooks early on. They have a natural interest and watch everything very carefully. Your Capricorn toddler will hate being fed by you. You use a spoon, knife and fork; they want exactly the same. So even if food goes all over the place let them at it with a spoon to feed themselves.

They are naturally tidy and will keep their rooms in very neat order. They hate muddles and dirt. Their clothes manage to stay cleaner longer. They enjoy a soapy bath. Listen out for that deep Capricorn chuckle as they mess about in the bath bubbles.

They are good at learning and enjoy it. They show an appetite for work from a very early age. School can be fun for them once they have settled in. Very young Capricorns can be quite shy and reserved. Whilst they are completely natural and friendly at home they can clam up as soon as a stranger comes into the house. They will probably draw very close to the mother and even turn their head away so that they don't even have to look at the newcomer. It would be very unlikely that they would speak to even the friendliest stranger.

Because they have an aptitude for work they learn easily at school once they have overcome their shyness and adapted to new surroundings. It won't happen quickly. It could take until half-term in the infant's class before they have entirely taken to the idea of going every single day. They enjoy success. They like to achieve.

If the house is neat — clean with a well-ordered routine — your little Capricorn will flourish in early childhood and grow into a solid, stable member of the school society. They will probably have just one best friend and a couple of acquaintances. They don't need or want a lot of friends. If anyone asked them who their best friend is, they would probably say it is their own mother.

From quite early on you will notice that they are good at taking care of their possessions and they are even aware of the value of money. They choose wisely and spend carefully. Although they want to fit in and do what all the other children are doing, they won't be joining in any bad behaviour. They seem to have a built-in mechanism that tells them that bad behaviour is wrong and not the direction they want to go in. They like adult approval and that includes the teacher's. If the teacher said a cross word to them they would take it very seriously and be very upset.

In your Capricorn you have a hard-working, friendly and very co-operative child.

SCORPIO babies are quite unforgettable. They have a beautiful, intense look in their eyes. You have the feeling that they have been on earth many times before, seen it all before and have landed back bringing centuries of wisdom with them. Little Scorpios pick up on the moods of the home much more quickly than other signs. They are emotionally in tune with everything that is happening around them. They have a natural sympathy with the other figure. Moods are sensed and silent support is given by the Scorpio child. You'll think to yourself, *but how on earth did that child know, realise, and understand what was going on?* It's just that they do, that's all. This is one of the most intuitive signs of the zodiac.

They can be a bit finicking when it comes to food. Don't dump a big plateful of food in front of them. Offer them tiny portions of miniature foods that have real appeal for them.

They like school because it gives them a chance to meet new people. They are curious about and interested in new people. They like watching them, listening to them and finding out how they think. Your little Scorpio will come home from school and announce that they have a boyfriend or girlfriend. They are fascinated by and fascinating to the opposite sex from a very early age. This is the mental explorer of the zodiac; they want to find out everything about everything.

The teacher is the power source in the classroom. They are influenced by a good teacher. A lot of adult Scorpions will recall one teacher who had the greatest influence on them in childhood. New words intrigue them. They like repeating them, finding out what they mean.

Don't expect them to get too involved in sports. Scorpios are well made and move easily, and they can be quite competitive, but they are not very sports oriented. If your little Scorpio is a bit down or seems to be in a melancholy mood, put some music on and watch them dance. They have a magical response to music and from very early childhood are brilliant dancers. They come to life listening to music. They have a natural rhythm, making them happy dancers.

Scorpios discover a talent or ambition quite early in life. I've known Scorpios of six or seven state clearly what they want to do as an adult. Then they work towards a goal, often achieving it early on. They are drawn to power and powerful positions. They like money and have an adult understanding of the power of money. It's not just about buying sweets or toys. Money can influence other people.

The Scorpio child won't show hurt feelings. It would be hard to know sometimes what they are thinking about. You can safely bet that they are thinking, sometimes deeply, about what has gone on in the day. They like to make sense of things.

As they get older, say from seven onwards, they become conscious of their power to charm. If the Scorpio decides to use their charm and flirtation skills to get their own way, it always works. They never go overboard. This is after all, a fairly disciplined sign, and they really don't like overdone emotions. There is a sense of refinement in Scorpions.

Even as a young child they absolutely love going on holiday, and they are very easy to please. A day at the seaside, a picnic on a mountain side, a swim in a river or natural pool is wonderful for them. That happy memory will live with them forever. A foreign holiday is pure magic. They are instantly enchanted by a foreign language. By the end of the holiday you'll find them speaking with a foreign accent and trying to learn and repeat some of the new and exciting words they have heard.

You'll also see that your finicking little eater at home is eating huge amounts of foreign food as though it was the food of the gods.

A loveable and unforgettable child.

ARIES are supposed to be the human dynamos of the zodiac. Perhaps they are in later childhood, but I have found over the years that the tiny Arian is quite timid. They love being at home. They are quite brave and bold in their own small world. You might find that they have disappeared, and are to be found in the garden digging, scraping and covered in muck. Or they might have been watching a spider spinning a web. They can be quite solitary as very young children. From early on they will have their favourite television programmes and feel very put out if they have to miss a favourite show. They frown and pout and fold their arms across their chest, really showing you how aggrieved they are. They like their possessions and detest anyone touching their things. Money is important. They like money. They count it and hide it away and if anyone dares touch either their money or their possessions they are treated to the famous Arian temper. No one, but no one, is in any doubt about their feelings of injustice and outrage.

They like having pets around and can be physically quite fearless even with large dogs that make other children or even adults quite wary.

Yet when it comes to starting school they are fearful and nervous. They don't like it one little bit. They would much rather stay at home on their own patch. They will probably stay very, very quiet in school, even when the teachers speak to them. They reason that if they don't speak, the teacher won't know that they are there. They don't have a lot of natural patience so learning to read and write comes slowly to them.

As soon as they get home, school is forgotten immediately, and when reminded that homework has to be done, they are surprised and again aggrieved. No one does the aggrieved bit quite as well as the Arian child.

When they make friends and discover the fun side of school they really begin to enjoy it. If there is a school uniform they take pride in wearing it and by the time they are ten or eleven they like their clothes to be clean, pressed and just a little bit different. They develop a keen and witty sense of humour and when that solemn face breaks into a smile it really is the most lovely transformation.

Sports and Aries go hand in hand. Once your Arian child has discovered a sport he or she likes they feel as though they have come home. They are naturally athletic, spend less time in front of the television and dream, eat and talk sport. They have a favourite team they follow, and wear team colours with pride. They like to model their own behaviour on that of the current sporting hero.

Aries is a brave and feisty child and you always know exactly where you are with them.

AQUARIUS children baffle their poor parents. The parents don't know what the child is thinking or what they are likely to do next. If you find your car has been run into the gate post, start your enquiries with the whereabouts and activities of your four year old Aquarian. They'll know something about it. If the timer on the oven is suddenly not working, it's likely that your little Aquarian was trying to find out how it worked. Aquarians aren't destructive, they are creators, but they have a massive curiosity about the world they occupy. They want to know everything. In school, they can be the wild card in the pack. They may not settle, may not adapt to the discipline of the classroom, yet their mathematics applied to weighing, measuring and timing is faultless. They are always active, always investigating, exploring, doing something. They also have an in-built sense of direction. If you're in a strange city or on holiday with a little Aquarian and can't find your way back to the hotel or apartment block let your little Aquarian guide you. You won't be led astray.

They are loveable children but not very cuddly. If you try to hug them they will usually strain away, seeming impatient. They aren't rejecting you, that's just the way they are made.

People observe that young children can astound their parents by asking deep and searching questions. Those people are talking about Aquarian children. They are very deep thinkers from an early age. Don't feel offended if your young Aquarian points out a more efficient way for you to do the housework, cook a meal or find a better place to get the car serviced. It's all part of that deep and logical thought process. Get used to it because it's going to last a lifetime in which your Aquarian child will take you on a marvellous journey of discovery. They are very easy children who practically bring themselves up.

TAUREAN babies are sturdy, placid and very attractive. They don't like to be hurried in anything. They feed slowly, often falling asleep two or three times. As they grow into toddlerhood they show very definite preferences for food and little Taurus simply won't eat (no matter how persuasive and cajoling you try to be) foods that they don't like. They like as many savoury foods as sweet ones and seem to have a natural aversion to junk food. They eat small amounts very slowly and are often very hungry first thing in the morning and again late at night.

They notice clothes and have favourite outfits. One top or jacket can be pretty much the same as the next — you think. But little Taurus has noticed the difference. They make it impossible to dress them in clothes that don't appeal by stiffening their arms. This silent resistance is the key to their personality. If they don't want or don't like something, they will just resist. Taurus has the strongest will in the zodiac. Go along with them and you have a delightful and warm hearted child. They make friends easily and their friends are very important to them. These children are very sociable.

They like a firm routine and if a bedtime story is part of that routine they are in heaven. They hang onto and remember every word of the story, so don't even think about skipping a page.

Taureans need a huge amount of attention. Try watching a television show you love with little Taurus in the room. That's the moment they will want to sit on your lap for a cuddle and a chat. Same thing will happen if a friend calls around for a cup of coffee and a bit of gossip.

Taurean children loathe conflict and if you and your dearly beloved are having a set-to, your child will tell you to stop. And there is no doubting the authority in that small firm voice. More than with any other sign you can see clearly the adult that this child will become.

The ♐ **SAGITTARIUS** baby is the chatterbox of the zodiac. Most Sagittarian children learn to talk very early. Some even try to teach themselves to read before they have started school. They are quick, alert, and are born with the belief that their place is everywhere. If you and other adults are having a discussion, expect your little Sagittarian to join in. If you tell them to scram they are highly offended. They are much more than observers and they like giving advice. Sagittarian children are very restless, finding it impossible to keep still for very long. They laugh a lot and from very early on have a ready sense of humour and drama. They enjoy recounting what happened in school that day, adding a few extra details for dramatic effect.

It is rare for a Sagittarian child to have many difficulties in school. They usually love the adventure of learning, of sports and any group activities. They are very sociable and collect things: friends, hobbies, toys. They seem to be always fiddling about with things and not really concentrating, but they are in fact picking up and absorbing a huge amount of knowledge very quickly. It gets stored away and is produced later when needed.

Childhood ailments seem to pass them by with remarkable ease. They appear cheerful and unaffected by most things going on around them. But if there are regular rows in the home, they suffer from earaches a lot. Apart from that they are physically strong and often test their physical strength beyond endurance. They are great little sports people and enjoy team and individual games and have an in-built sense of fair play. For them it really is the game that counts as they can handle losing with ease.

They usually have a sense quite early on of what job they want to do as an adult. As they grow towards adulthood they never quite lose their endearing childhood qualities of openness, honesty and the unfailing ability to put their foot into it, time and again.

♊ **GEMINI** baby is cute, with wide-open eyes that sparkle with interest and amusement. Gemini baby has a joy about being alive that they communicate to the whole wide world. They gurgle and chuckle long before they talk and seem to make so many attempts to communicate just about every emotion under the sun, that it truly amazes their wide and admiring circle of onlookers. From the very alert expression in their eyes they seem to understand every single thing that is said to them. The truth of this is quickly apparent when they do start talking, which is very early, because they use a very wide vocabulary. Parents often wonder how on earth the tiny child learned so many words. Gemini records words as soon as they are heard and, understanding them fully, is able to repeat them in accurate context in very early toddlerhood. It's no wonder so many journalists and media people come from this sign. They often have lovely singing voices and take great joy from music, playing an instalment and singing. Little Geminis seem to have a natural stage presence and can act and entertain even as very small children. They know very well how to captivate an audience by being enchanting and clever.

Despite their cleverness, Gemini children don't always do as well at school as parents expect. They are very restless with a short concentration span. When expected to sit still and study or do homework they get very impatient. They have brains, but not much real interest in academic work and they often under-achieve, sometimes leaving school at the earliest possible opportunity. In an ideal world they should be encouraged to take early education as far as they choose to go, leave school, go out into the world and do five or six different jobs before returning to full-time education as a mature student.

🦁 LEO children are born with quite astonishing good looks and large, serious eyes. They command, even in infanthood, with a strong and dominating personality. They need and expect a huge amount of attention and get it. There can sometimes be problems with brothers and sisters because of this. Leo commands and demands every scrap of attention and doesn't always see that it is at the expense of siblings. Yet, Leos also manage to command immense family loyalty. They are at their best with pets. Pets are good for Leos, because they bring out all the soft and tender qualities in that great big Leo heart. Even very small Leo children take a great and deep interest in wildlife, animals and nature. They love going to the zoo and studying the animals. They look at picture books and photos of birds, beasts and fish in their natural habitat.

They like watching sport and are emotionally moved by great sporting moments such as a horse race, a football or soccer match and they admire heroic performances. They read avidly from an early age.

Leo children often have deep and beautiful voices. They may not say very much, but what they do say is beautifully said and very well articulated. They don't have much time for small talk. They go to the heart of the matter.

Life is an art form for Leo. They love beautiful things; designed gardens, attractively matched colours and an appealingly-laid table. Their tastes are shown very early in life. Their big eyes light up appreciatively when they see good quality food. All these tastes are instincts, because no one has explained to the three year old about good manners and good taste, yet Leo has it all.

I have seen small Leos attempt to cook. They are always good cooks, yet a lot of Leos will say that they hate cooking and do it rarely. Yet, when they do it is superb. Typically a small Leo will experiment with making some dish or other and eat and admire the results while the family is left cleaning the large mess they left behind.

They can be incredibly stubborn and they feel deep resentment if forced to do something against their will. In school they might be fairly solitary, but won't either bully or be bullied. They have a natural sense of what is right and wrong and always try to do the right thing. The friends they make in infant's class are few; usually only one boy and one girl, but they will remain faithful to those friends through thick and thin. In the course of a long life I have almost never known a Leo child to tell a lie. They are sound children who grow into very sound adults.

CANCERIAN children cry a lot. They are soft, sentimental and very easily hurt. Mother is the centre of the Cancerian child's world. Cancerians adore their mothers, they put them on a pedestal, work hard to earn their approval, bond quickly, easily and permanently. Little Cancerians are so loving and affectionate that they break many hearts. They radiate an innocent joy and one cross word or frown could wound them deeply. They cry or retreat into hurt silence, puzzled that anyone should disapprove of them. They parent younger brothers and sisters with a strong protective love that sometimes make them seem a little bossy.

To the Cancerian child school is not the most welcoming place in the world. They are quite happy in the kitchen at home, running confidently around, knowing and loving every nook and cranny. The familiar sights and smells are very dear to them; they hate leaving it behind. I can't think of one little Cancerian I know who hasn't wept at parting from their mother at the classroom door.

To make it easier, take the walk to school a good few times before schol starts, finding nice and interesting things en route to look at and talk about. Get the Cancerian to help you pack their lunch box. That way, there is a direct connection between the kitchen table and the classroom. Expect to hear a tale of woe every day when the child comes home, for at least the first week. Gradually school will become as familiar and nearly as much loved as home. But because the Cancerian is essentially loving and loveable they soon make friends and look forward to seeing them every day.

In very early childhood they show the qualities that they take into adulthood; kindness, care of others and deep, tender and protective love.

♎ **LIBRA** baby is a beauty; a very good-looking child, with big eyes, long slender limbs and a dazzling smile. They know they are the pet of the family and they absolutely love it. Libras thrive on love and attention. But they don't abuse this position as they are hard workers. You'll never have to tell your Libran child twice to tidy a room or put their things away. They like starting school early as they love having friends to chat to. They can converse about anything as soon as they are able to talk. Parents become conscious that the little Libran isn't just babbling, or repeating, they are actually making conversation.

Produce a camera and watch young Libra perform; they smile directly into the lens, pose and just love it. Librans aren't shy but they can be quite reserved at times. Librans have a quality of finesse about them from a very young age. They aren't snobs but they don't like coarse or loutish behaviour. If a friend in the road or at school pushes other children around, uses bad language or behaves badly, the little Libran will drop them very quickly. They are very lucky children because they are influenced by good behaviour and good taste and repelled by bad things.

Don't ask them what they want to eat, (unless they are vegetarian — and a lot of Libran children are naturally vegetarian) just put the food on the table. If you ask them they will either change their mind a hundred times or won't be able to make it up at all. Give them loads of time for getting ready to go out because they will spend a lot of time thinking about what to wear or changing an outfit several times. You'll do your Libran and yourself a huge favour if you get them into a school with a uniform or school dress code. You'll both be spared the agony of Libran indecision. It's the same with birthday or Christmas presents. Choice is agony — they can't decide on what they want.

Hand even a very small Libran a problem and they will agonise, trying to see it from every point of view before coming up with an answer.

They make friends with and stay friends with brothers and sisters and never take them for granted. Their kindness and good manners aren't a party piece reserved for outsiders. It starts with and stays with members of their own family. These wonderful and attractive children grow into wonderful and attractive adults.

♊ **VIRGO** baby is really cute to look at, with a solemn expression, soulful eyes, and a quirky smile. Virgo baby needs lots of physical attention, cuddles, soothing talk and nursing. For some reason, Virgo babies tend to get colic more ofter than other babies. Despite this, they have a good appetite and only develop finicky food habits as they get a bit older. You'll notice two things about your Virgo toddler: One is that they have an amazing ability to concentrate. Great attention, a slightly frowning gaze, and silence, reign as Virgo toddler takes a good, long look at the environment. Everything is noticed. Movements can be quite still, and little sound is made. It is easy to see from the expression in little Virgo's eyes that their surroundings are being mentally measured, every detail being stored away in their very active brain. The next thing noticeable is the way the Virgo child organises everything. As soon as they can walk and pick up things, everything has a place. The Virgo child has a very good memory and sense of direction. Anything can be located very quickly. That sense of order remains with the Virgo child.

From six or seven onwards, the Virgo child likes to keep the room clean and orderly. Muddles and dirt actually unsettle them very much and make them irritable. Young Virgoans also have a sense of justice and fair play, and are among those who will say with a real sense of passion that something or other is not fair.

Naturally well-mannered, the Virgoan child is usually easy to manage. Stubbornness and a bad-temper only appear if the Virgoan child feels that not enough attention is being paid to them, or that the adult is not listening to what they say. It is said that adults should never make a promise to a child if they have no intention of keeping it. This is especially true of Virgoan children. They will feel a real sense of grievance over a promise made and not kept. It will be pointed out at intervals over the following few years.

Carers of Virgoans need to explain to them through words, stories and drama that adults have their failings, that the world is not a perfect place and that sometimes promises are made in perfectly good faith but later cannot be delivered. The Virgoan understands and accepts when the explanation has been given. The Virgoan child thinks a great deal about all sorts of things, and builds theories about how the world and people work.

It always comes as a surprise that so serious a child can have a wonderful sense of humour and a ready and infectious chuckle. Virgo children also respond to music, and when encouraged to sing, develop a good singing voice and ear for music early on.

Monitor your Virgoan in school. They are intelligent and hard workers, but can sometimes be very sensitive if something goes wrong. They may believe that the teacher does not appreciate their efforts, or that other children get a fairer deal in the classroom. An out of school activity like sport, music or drama is emotionally healthy for Virgo children.

If, at any point, your Virgo child stops working in school, go in and find out why. There will be a reason. Laziness won't be it, because Virgoan children are hard-working, and that work ethic is not only natural but a lifetime activity.

PISCES baby believes in magic, and it would have to be a heartless parent who wouldn't deliver that wonderful quality into this baby's life. Pisceans are babies; small, needy, trusting and believing. They hold up baby arms, expecting to be picked up and hugged and petted. They open eyes wide and beautiful to a world they firmly believe will deliver all and everything to them that they want and need. Pisceans don't need much — only love, warmth and protection. Piscean toddlers talk endlessly, expect a loving response, and that touch of magic. They will hold their breath as you tell them a fairy story. They know that there are fairies and magical beings in their world. These are the children who believe in Santa Claus longer than any other children. The day they find out that Santa Claus does not exist is the saddest day of their lives. They want and live in a wonderland where parents are perfect, the sun will always shine and everyone else wants all the good and perfect things they crave. They can sing, dance and act. Sometimes parents put them into acting classes believing that the Piscean child wants a hobby or a career on the stage. Not so. Piscean children sing, dance and act as part of their natural personalities. They are artistic and creative. Again, that's a natural part of their personality.

They have very lively imaginations and if any child has an imaginary friend they talk to, it's likely to be a Piscean child. School is a big adventure for these children. If they can stop for long enough, they get a fair bit of learning done. But play is what they are best at. Life is a game to them, a game without too many restrictions and rules. They are so spontaneous that rules don't fit in with their fun agenda. They are not one bit selfish or self-centred. Pisceans enjoy sharing their time, possessions and food with other children. They attract lots of friends because they are naturally friendly and sociable. Loneliness and boredom are almost unknown to them because with their lively and inventive mind they can always think of something to do.

When given a new task they can show a bit of reluctance. They need to be led by the hand and told exactly what is expected of them and how to do it. Say for instance, you want to teach them how to use a computer or use the telephone, give them lots of praise for what they do right and ignore any mistakes. Keep patiently repeating what has to be done, reinforcing instructions with praise and encouragement until they are confident enough to work alone. Even in adult life Pisceans shy away from new tasks, and I can't think of a single Piscean who can fill out a form without making at least one mistake. Yet, when given more difficult or abstract tasks, such learning to tell the time, little Pisceans do well. Even though Pisces is a water sign, a lot of Piscean children don't like water and can't swim.

When your Pisces child smiles they really do bring a precious ray of sunshine into the room and into your life.

Taming The Teenager

PISCES is one of the easiest signs to get along with and is unlikely to give too many headaches during their teenage years. Pisces thrives on loving approval. As a teenager some of that approval comes from the opposite sex. Pisces is quite open about relationships so parents know all about newcomers in their childrens' lives. But Pisces is attracted to the very people their parents do not approve of. Parents blame Pisces' sudden lack of interest in their studies on the newcomer, claiming that the newcomer is a bad influence. Parents are then really surprised at Pisces' defence of their love choice and their total refusal to give the relationship up.

TEEN TIP: *Don't show disapproval of a teenage relationship.*

ARIES love their teens and enters into just about every teen activity. Their parents are cast aside and they don't see their parents as having the remotest understanding of their new world, friends and activities. They can become distant and spend hours going off on a sporting jaunt with new friends. Aries resent parental questions, which they regard as quite pointless as parents couldn't understand the thrill, and excitement they have discovered. They regard their discovery of

147

sex, booze and music as entirely their own. They revel in their new-found independence.

TEEN TIP: *Don't ask too many questions, but make it clear you need some idea of their whereabouts.*

♎ **LIBRA** will fall in love and whilst they still love their parents and cherish their approval, it's no longer necessary; they have all the approval they need from the partner with whom they fall completely in love with. They may even want to leave school early to show that they are as completely and fully in love as Romeo and Juliet.

TEEN TIP: *Take their love affair very seriously, pointing out that the partner deserves a Libran who is educated to support the relationship for a lifetime.*

♊ **GEMINI** feels that parents won't approve or understand why they flirt with half-a-dozen partners, experiment with smoking, drink or the odd drug. They will carry on acting in the home in the way that their parents expect. They certainly will keep their activities secret. But as most of these activities are kept well away from home, they may want to leave home early.

TEEN TIP: *Show a friendly interest but insist that you need to know their whereabouts. Encourage them to bring new friends home.*

TAURUS goes through unexpected mood swings and makes a determined attempt not to show parents that they have changed. For a lot of Taureans physical change happens quickly. It surprises and even scares them a bit, but they'll never admit it. They hide their fears beneath a surly mask and often retreat to brood. From peer group reaction they discover that they have a magnetism for the opposite sex. After the initial surprise they begin to enjoy it, but continue to hide changes in themselves until they have understood and accepted it. They often swing back from time to time looking for the certainties and reassurances of the childhood state.

TEEN TIP: *Don't respond to surly moods, just make it clear that it's easier to get along with everyone if good manners and polite speech are the order of the day.*

CANCER: These attractive teenagers give very little trouble. They accept all the friendship and camaraderie and freedom available to them. Yet, parental approval remain very important to them..

TEEN TIP: *Give firm and uncompromising guidance on drink and drugs.*

AQUARIUS is a constantly evolving person and the process of becoming a teenager probably began at nine or ten. They have been curious about everything, exploring everything and they may have older friends amongst their large circle of friends. They aren't going to be influenced against their will by anyone. They keep their head, focus and balance, both at school and in their social life.

TEEN TIP: *Keep lines of communication open and listen because they'll tell you everything anyway.*

🐾 **CAPRICORN** might worry you by appearing to become a loner and burying themselves in work. They have schoolwork, plan a college career and probably have a part-time job. You'll wonder why they aren't giddy like other teenagers, chasing after love at discos. They may even appear wise beyond their years.

TEEN TIP: *Convince them to take up a hobby; preferably a group activity like drama, politics, or a photography club.*

🎇 **SAGITTARIUS** enjoys going wild. Sagittarians are convinced that their parents are in need of their advice and guidance. They know how to convince parents that they are leading a life of unparalleled saintliness. They don't want to talk about what's going on in their lives, not because they are doing anything to be ashamed of but because they are developing an adult privacy important to them and they don't want freedom curbed.

TEEN TIP: *Don't deny them adult privileges if you want them to take on adult responsibilities.*

🦁 **LEO** teenagers want and usually have a great time. They enter into everything: the dressing up, the socialising, the long hours gossiping and listening to music. They want to go on holiday abroad with friends and they need a lot of your money to do this, since their busy schedule doesn't allow them much time to work. They can also be quite aggressive towards parents who attempt to limit their freedom.

TEEN TIP: *Don't take aggressive or rude responses to your questions. Expect them to get a part-time job to pay for their expensive lifestyle.*

🦂 **SCORPIO** is naturally secretive. They don't like parting with information and are convinced that parents don't understand life. You won't stop your Scorpio from sampling one affair after another, but you'll wound them deeply if you suggest that it's just about sex and not romance. They'll manage school or college work very competently. They won't argue with you, or openly defy you, but they won't tell you a tenth of what's going on. You'll need to be a bit of a private detective to find out.

TEEN TIP: *Don't intrude too much on their privacy and state clearly what they need to do to stay safe. Be entirely practical and non-judgemental.*

♍ **VIRGO** can transform overnight from a model, compliant and loveable child, always anxious to please, into a raving revolutionary. A distinct fashion style is adopted. They adopt the language of the peer group. Parents are treated with disdain. A big distance can develop between parents and their Virgo child. Their rebellious views are announced with triumphant defiance. It tempts many baffled and unhappy parents to agree with the Virgoan teen for the sake of peace.

TEEN TIP: *Re-state rules calmly but repetitively, because Virgo desperately needs the reassurance.*

Dealing With Loss

———————

Sometimes when a person comes for a reading they might warn me in advance that they don't want to hear any bad news, particularly about death. At that point I usually push a piece of blank paper and a pen across the desk and ask them to write down a list of people they know will never die. They take the paper and start to ply the pen, then they stop, frown and return the paper to me, accepting the fact that everyone must die. It is the only certainty we have. The only forecast we can make about life is that it will end in death.

Bereavement is always difficult. No pill can make it easier; it only delays the natural and inevitable feelings that are part of being human. Some people appear to recover and deal with bereavement quite easily, although what most people mean when they say that the bereaved person is coping well is that they are not embarrassing others by a show of emotion. In the face of bereavement there really is little to say, except to offer comfort and a sympathetic ear. Coping with the death of a dearly loved one reveals the strengths and weaknesses of each sign. Even when the death is expected, after, say a long illness, it still comes as a shock. A door has closed that will never open again.

🐏 **ARIES** appears to cope really well. Aries won't talk much about the death or the dead person. They go on much as before, working, shopping, cleaning the house, paying the bills, clinging to a routine that is known and comfortable. If anyone close attempts to raise the subject of death, loss or sadness, Aries will brush it to one side, as though they have accepted the fact of death and have no wish to talk about it. They may even say that there is nothing to talk about. If offered bereavement counselling they would most likely refuse it. The feelings of grief and shock are buried away quickly as though Aries is frightened to examine them too closely. It sometimes takes Aries a couple of years before they can talk about their feelings. It takes them that long to adjust to the idea that the dead person is not coming back, and to understand just how important a part the dead person played in their life. After a couple of years they have a complete picture of the person, the good points, and the not so good. It's only when they have that completed picture can they open up and talk about deep or disturbing feelings. Death and the reaction to that death can often be a very healing process for Aries. They emerge from it with more wisdom and maturity than they ever thought they possessed.

🏹 **SAGITTARIUS** is sometimes a flippant and jovial sign. Often Sagittarians appear not to take life too seriously and can make a joke on most subjects. It is their own way of coping. They often deny feelings of sadness. That is not a strength, it is often a weakness. But in deep grief their very real feelings shoot to the surface. They are taken by surprise and humbled in the face of an onslaught of grief and sadness they scarcely knew existed. Completely overwhelmed, they experience a massive fatigue and want to take to bed for a week to recover some physical vitality. They begin a quest for some meaning to death, some reassurance that there is life after death, that there is some sort of continuity, some point to it all.

Some Sagittarians cannot accept death, but these are few. Most Sagittarians accept death as a natural part of life. They miss the dead person with all the physicality of this sign, but don't wish for the person back. They talk a lot during bereavement. It helps them more than anything else to deal with feelings of sadness and loss. They look at photographs, go to places where they were once happy, visit the grave every day, write letters to the departed person. Activity and talk are great therapies for Sagittarians. After three months life begins to right itself. They truly understand that time heals.

TAURUS grieves for a very long time. Taureans love very deeply and find letting go a very hard business. People they love become part of them. The love they feel for close and dear ones survives the grave for years and years. They don't want the possessions touched. They get great comfort by turning the dead person's room into a sort of shrine. They go frequently to the grave with flowers and cards. Remembering and respecting the dead is part of birthdays and Christmas. They pray for the dead, if they are religious, or support the relevant medical charity if the dead person died, for instance, from cancer or heart disease. They cannot bear anyone to talk disrespectfully or irreverently of the dead person, although they themselves may not talk about the death or their feelings at all. Everything, all their love and grief, is carried around in that great big Taurean heart. Small things can trigger the grief, keeping it as fresh as the first day it was experienced.

CAPRICORN people accept death and learn to live with it peacefully and easily. It is something they have thought about and not pushed to the back of the mind in the hope it will never happen. Of all the signs, Capricorn is the most accepting of the fact that everybody eventually will die and that death is natural and inevitable. It reveals the spiritual side of their nature and personality not normally on view to anyone outside their immediate circle. Capricorn is a wonderful person to talk to if you are weighed down with the burden of grief. Grieving brings out all that is soft and humane in the Capricorn character. Capricorns fully understand their own grief and that of people around them. They understand that it has its own time, and in its own time will fade to the background of life. Somehow Capricorn normalises grief, if that is possible, and makes it a normal part of life.

AQUARIUS searches for the dignity in death, examining the possibility of life after death and the place of each and every one of us, dead and alive, in the great scheme of things. Being one of the great thinkers of the zodiac – Aquarius has usually given a lot of thought to death, amongst many other things — so that the idea or fact of death is neither strange nor terrifying. There is always a faint other-worldly quality about most Aquarians. They know that the soul survives the earthly state and the spirit of the dead person is never far away. For comfort in bereavement the Aquarian reaches out and feels the presence close, warm and loving. Aquarians are not so lost in their own grief that they cannot recognise the state of the living around them and give endless hope and encouragement to other bereaved members of their family.

GEMINI has a rationale about death and can talk about it. Gemini is also very good at talking about emotions and can identify exactly what those emotions are. Talking about grieving is a very healthy and important part of the way Gemini copes with and survives bereavement. Gemini also has many loyal and loving friends to whom she has been supportive and they rally around during her grieving. Gemini women will talk, weep and allow to flow out all that hurt and those negative emotions. After about three months she is emotionally spent, but in a calm and peaceful space. In this space she is able to become, once again, the counsellor of others needing her help. Her sense of humour returns, and her analytical mind helps her to get an accurate, even unsentimental picture of the person who has passed away. She won't create a static shrine or allow herself to be held emotionally in a state of loss. Her energy returns and she allows life to reclaim her. She loves the business of living and this triumphs over sadness. She is able to move on because life, for her, is about being on the move.

CANCER women are overcome by bereavement. They close in on themselves, and retreat into their own private world. Talking about loss does not come easily to this sign. Their home, and circle of family and friends, is dear to Cancer and at the very core of her being. The loss of someone close affects every moment of every day. Habits are changed, routine is different, emotional ties cannot be transferred. Every memory, every photograph, every date of significance relating to the lost person is agonised over, again and again. The world without that dear face is a bleak and unbearable place. In that private place of bleakness, Cancer suffers the deepest agony of loss. Cancerian women find it unbearably difficult to articulate the depth of their grief. Words are few, the facial expression bland, almost immobile. The first flowers of spring are greeted with sadness because the dead person is not there to share the joy with the lonely and bereft Cancerian.

Christmas or any other calendar event of celebration is anticipated with dread because everything will be different. Visiting the grave will be done privately, even secretly, because Cancer finds it difficult to share with others the feelings that belong to her. There is almost a jealous guarding of feelings, because they are the exclusive domain of the Cancerian and her dead. She resents any intrusion. Her bodily needs become neglected and she may lose weight and sleep. Grief creeps inexorably towards depression and it may take many months, even a couple of years, before normal feelings return.

When someone close to her dies, a part of Cancer woman dies too. What draws her back to life is the birth of a child for someone close, or maybe someone needing her caring skills. She will return to join the land of the living, but she needs time and a lot of very patient love.

LEO, in many ways, appears to react in the same way as Cancer to death, but the underlying emotions are different. Leo is frozen by strong emotions. Sometimes, in the early days of bereavement, they are completely overwhelmed and sometimes suffer physical aches and muscle spasms. Occasionally their body seems to seize up, making it difficult to move. An overwhelming fatigue dominates the mind and body and many Leos take to bed and stay there. Others close to them think it is depression, but it is the complete inability to function and move off the shocked spot that causes the mental and physical reaction.

Gradually, as the shock departs, the physical symptoms ease away and Leo accepts the death has taken place. The picture of life gradually resumes normality. Talking will be done with those Leo completely trusts and loves. This happens two or three months after the death. For a short time, a compulsive and dependent relationship forms between Leo and the person in whom she is confiding. Then Leo is able to recover physically and mentally and resume normal living in the calm acceptance of the loss of a loved one.

The sadness and sense of loss remains but becomes a natural part of their mental and physical life. It adds a richness in their relationships with other people. Death and grieving become a valuable dimension to their daily life. Bereavement deepens awareness in Leos. They come through the process a much stronger person.

Leo grows, is kinder, less judgmental, more willing to enter into other people's deeply felt emotions about life and death. They emerge from grieving a finer and stronger person. They see the frailty of people like Virgo.

But ✿ **VIRGO** suffers in bereavement because all those rules that make life a comfortable and ordered business suddenly don't work any more. The person they have loved is gone. The key turning in the lock at six o'clock every evening won't be heard again. Any resentments or irritations they had about the dead person become instantly erased from the conscious mind. The very flaws and imperfections that drove them mad when the person was alive suddenly become dearly loved traits viewed with tolerance and affection. They long for another chance at life with that person; to say how sorry they are for nagging or for showing intolerance. Poor Virgo suffers the agony of grief and the agony of guilt. Every single Virgoan fault is magnified and dwelt on with deep remorse. Virgo can't find a single fault in the dead person or a single virtue in the self.

Everything is questioned, even the existence of an after-life. But the spirituality that is a deep and abiding part of the Virgoan nature begins to surface. They are kinder and more understanding of others. They listen attentively to those who keep faith with them, reminding them of their own loving goodness. Belief in the self returns. Belief in the rightness of universal order returns. Belief in one's own essential goodness and justness returns. Virgo is in its truest essence an earth sign. There are seasons, beginnings and endings. Death is not an enemy but the natural completion of the life-cycle. Every honour and respect is paid to the dead person. There is a natural Virgoan dignity brought to bear on the funeral rites and the memorials to the dead person. In carrying out these rites of passage, the Virgoan has begun their own healing.

The first anniversary of the dead person becomes a celebration of the life that has passed on. It is a relief to Virgo as she realises that her own life has by then resumed its normal state.

She finds it a bit difficult to understand LIBRA, who seems to handle bereavement in a completely different way.

ꙮ **LIBRA** woman's moods seem to swing from deepest grief into hilarity as she recalls some amusing incident in the life of the dead person. Libra woman feels death completely and instantly. There is an immediate knowledge that the person will never return. There is no looking up every time the door opens, as though in expectation. But the photographs are taken out, the best framed and displayed. The dead person will be grieved over but never forgotten. They have joined the ranks of honoured but dead forebears of the family or circle of friends.

Libra won't build a shrine to the dead person; she will dispose of the possessions and clothes when she is ready. She will keep only the possessions to which she has her own sentimental attachments. They will belong in her treasure box and will be brought out and talked about. She won't suffer the agonies of a remorseful conscience about the things she should have done when that person was alive, because she knows that she was never anything but kind, loving and attentive. That comforts her. She has an instinct about life beyond the grave and knows that love cannot end at the grave. She also feels that she will one day meet that person again. The parting is only temporary. Their ways will join again. She'll catch up on all the news and gossip. Her normally joyful love of life will again surface. She has all the support of the living and relies on it to see her through until she is once again able to cope with the business of living.

SCORPIO, like Libra, has an instinctive acceptance of death. Scorpio has thought about death and has wondered about the nature of life after death. Scorpio is prepared for death. Scorpio has more ability than any other sign of the zodiac to survive the deepest tragedy. Every life transition has been part of the process of death, ending, and re-birth. The deep feelings of personal loss are buried while Scorpio attempts to digest the passing of a loved one, and readjust to a different life.

It may seem to observers that Scorpio is handling the death well, even easily. But those deeply buried feelings begin to surface, and about six weeks after the death, the tough Scorpio body begins to react. The bodily centres of grieving — the liver and lungs — are affected. They might suffer a severe chest infection, or some problems with the liver. Scorpios demand physical attention for bodily ailments. Gradually, they may begin to discuss how they are actually feeling. Tears begin to flow in a steady and healing stream.

The Scorpio has a psychic awareness that the dead person has left some small but vital part of the spirit behind, and that it has entered into Scorpio. It could be that the Scorpio discovers their handwriting has changed a bit, or that they have developed some taste in food shared by the dead person, or that some part of that kindly dead person's approach to life is now shared by Scorpio. This connection between the living and dead is infinitely appreciated by Scorpios. It comforts, reassures and sustains them during all the times when memory and emotion threaten to overwhelm them.

Scorpio women who have had a happy marriage are likely to marry again, and sometimes what others may see as unreasonably quickly, because they want that happiness continued. They will love the new husband while continuing to love the dead one. Mourning is not continued for ever, but love is.

♒ **PISCES** is, like Scorpio; a water sign, but they react differently to death. Pisces likes fun, hates sickness, and has, unless there has been previous experience of grieving the death of a loved one, given little thought to death. It is the finality of death that shocks Pisces. There is no continuation of that person, no tomorrow in which that dead person can feature as part of Piscean life. Pisces struggles with grief and tries to make sense of death. Maybe for the first time Pisces attempts to unravel deep mysteries about death and life after death. Their feelings oppress them; concentration is impossible, work is difficult.

Many Pisceans try to blot out unbearable feelings with alcohol, anti-depressants, or sleeping tablets. The physical and mental pain ravages them. They blunder around in a dark world filled with pain. If the death was unexpected, Pisces goes into a state of deep shock. Even if the death was expected, and they either nursed the sick or stayed at the hospital bedside, the shock is still severe.

Waking on the morning after the death has occurred is like, to Piscean woman, waking to a landscape turned upside down by an earthquake. It is alien territory, and they feel it will never be the same again. But their natural kindness reacts to the kindness shown to them. They respond to it, feeling the quality of its healing. The love of those alive sustains them. Gradually they respond to the warmth of sunshine, the scent of flowers, the sound of music. The experience of grieving has been deeply spiritual and one from which they emerge lifted into a new and sustaining spiritual place. They go on more lovingly with the business of life and love, but they never forget. And most days, for the rest of their lives a thought, fleeting but restful, reminds them of the life they loved and still mourn.

Dream Secrets

———◆———

Your dreams are direct messages from your subconscious mind. You dream in code, so you need a little help in working out what the coded messages are about. You could get a dream analysis book, but I've listed a few common dreams relating to your love and emotional life as a guide.

You observe, listen and record things, events and impressions all the time when you are awake. The significance of certain things you see and hear may escape your conscious attention, but they don't escape your subconscious mind. That person you think is a good friend, who talks in such a friendly way and is so good to you and your family, may not be all she seems. Your subconscious mind picks up on all the small details you miss. These many small details are recorded, processed and fed back to you via your dreams.

It's complicated, of course, by the fact that we dream in code. I'm not too sure just why we do. I'm sure there is a scientific explanation somewhere, but I don't have it. Dreaming of death, for instance, isn't an omen of a death about to occur, but more likely serves to inform you that a state of affairs is about to come to an end. Say, for example, you dream of the death of a child; it could be your subconscious telling you to be aware of the fact that a child has gone through a change and no longer needs babying.

Sometimes we aren't always aware when that good friend of ours has really stopped being a good friend and has become jealous, manipulative or outright hostile. We carry on confiding things that, really, we should be keeping quiet about. Or, maybe that colleague of your partner who is always so nice to you is, in reality, after your man.

Maybe you've been wondering if your man is faithful to you, if he really loves you, if he will always stay with you. But your dreams might be telling you that he is all you want him to be. We all find it hard to admit that we might, ourselves, be at fault, and our subconscious very kindly reminds us — maybe by sending a message that we are being a school ma'am, or a dictator — that the fault lies within you.

CATS: to dream of a cat is an omen that you have a false or hostile influence close to you. Someone you think of as a trusted friend is actively trying to do you damage. If the cat in your dream bites you, then you have to face a situation where someone you like and trust is about to deliver a very nasty surprise, and the truth about the falseness of the friendship is about to be revealed. If you manage to chase the cat away, you'll expose the false friend, and even limit the damage considerably. If you are a cat lover, a cat breeder, or your pet is your best friend, then this dream doesn't have the significance I've described. Still, I'm always wary of cat dreams; they aren't friendly.

BLINDNESS: or something wrong with your eyes or eyesight, or maybe seeing something through a mist or fog, is a warning that you are being deceived. Wake up! Take stock of what is happening around you. Has someone been dropping hints that your partner is playing away? Start a bit of detective work to discover what is going on in your personal life, because this dream is a serious warning that all is not well.

KNIFE: these dreams, whether they involve a dagger, sword, ordinary table knife or carving knife, are not good dreams to have. They mean that your relationship is in serious trouble and a lot of work has to be put in if you want to save the partnership. A broken knife in a dream is telling you that you'll have to think seriously about parting company.

DROWNING: or maybe swimming in turbulent or muddy waters, is advising you that you may be in a relationship you don't understand. Maybe you're with someone you care for, but there are problems that might be very difficult to solve. This type of dream can also mean that your partner has to do a lot of work to help the relationship along.

BLOOD: is often a forewarning that someone is angry — maybe just about life, maybe with you — and that some very angry words are about to be exchanged. It's not all doom and gloom though, as some things are all the better for having an airing. It's what happens next that counts. Your dream is advising you to be ready to do a lot of listening to your partner's (or friend's, or family member's) grievances.

FIRE: dreams depend on how you saw the fire in the dream. A nice cosy fire is a lovely omen of peace and contentment, whereas a raging, out-of-control fire means that you are in a love situation that's getting out of control, and some very prompt action is needed to set things right.

FLOWERS: fresh and lovely in a dream are a lovely sign that all is well in your relationship.

PERFUME: especially if you are conscious of a strong sweet smell, is a lovely dream meaning that your partner really fancies you as well as loves you.

KISSING: dreams are always satisfying and mean that your partner loves you very much.

HAIR: is interesting in dreams. If you dream that your hair is lovely, shiny, and healthy, that means your love life is in a similar condition. But if you dream of colouring your hair, or going blonde, then you may have to re-think your current affair, because he may not be as sincere as you think, or hope.

FOOD: dreams also relate to your emotional life. If the food (fruit, vegetables, meat, bread, or any other good foods) are fresh and either look or taste nice, then that will be reflected in your love life. If there is something wrong with it, then you'll have to look again at your partner, and see what has to be put right.

THE COLOURS OF LOVE

———◆———

Everyone is colour-conscious and has a favourite colour. Obviously, you're going to wear colours you like and feel comfortable in. But certain colours attract love into your life more easily. Wear the colour that's right for your sign of the zodiac, and just see what an amazing difference it can make. You'll attract more friends and, hopefully, the right love interest.

≋ **PISCES** needs all the sea shades, from blues to greens. Light blues through to aquamarine, and that particular shade of bronze-green is like a love magnet on Pisceans.

⋙ **AQUARIUS** looks stunning in the deep shades of indigo blue, touches of silver, and loads of silver accessories.

⋙ **CAPRICORN** looks good in very dark green — just one colour — and a few bits of real gold accessories.

⋙ **ARIES** can wear very bright red. Even tiny Arians (and a lot of Arians are tiny in stature) can carry this bright colour. The fewer accessories the better; maybe one diamond, but not much more.

LIBRA looks sensational in white, with lots of silver and sapphire, or sapphire-coloured jewellery.

CANCER looks great in deep purple and black, with a great moonstone collar, or very high heeled, pearly-coloured boots.

TAURUS looks amazing in rich emeralds and ruby colours, with just one, very large, topaz pendant.

SAGITTARIUS should wear deep blue with amethyst bracelets, or a myriad of blues, greens, ambers and ruby red.

LEO can look good in royal blue, hyacinth, purple and pink, with gold and silver. This is probably the only sign able to wear gold and silver together and get away with it.

SCORPIO looks good in black, with silver accessories, looking stylish and sexy if matched with red patent stilettos.

GEMINI should wear loads of colour. Indeed, it is the only sign that can wear any colour at all, and the bigger the mixture the better. Rings with huge designs to match those large and sparkling Gemini eyes go down a treat.

✿ **VIRGO** looks great in olive green, with a tiny pinstripe, leather high heels, and a single stone ring of green onyx.

WORK & MONEY

Work & Money

When I first started my psychic radio show several years ago, a good proportion of the callers were asking about either serious financial problems, fearing that they might lose their job, or were just making enough to make ends meet. Now those calls are coming in again. A lot of people are not benefiting from the wealth that is being created in society. They are doing well if they can make ends meet and manage to save a bit. I am going to show you the strengths and weaknesses various people can have, sign by sign.

Some people seem born lucky. They inherit money, they win, or marry it. That's often linked to your star sign — and more often than you think.

Others run up debt. They don't know when to stop spending. The first priority is that if you are beginning to run into debt, STOP SPENDING! Some signs, like Sagittarius and Aquarius, are famed for their optimism. They always believe that something will turn up. But there is a defining moment when optimism becomes outright stupidity. What turns up is an even larger bill. The solution to the problem is that bit farther away. It has never made any sense to me that what you do when in debt is to take out yet another loan.

Often on radio and television I advise the individual or family to live on beans and chips for a month, and use the saved money to target the most pressing bill. That's not my naïvetè, or the draconian message it sounds like. To me, it makes sense.

A character in David Copperfield said that if a person earns a pound a week and spends nineteen shillings and six pence, that is perfect happiness. But if the earner of a pound a week spends twenty shillings and six pence, that's misery. It was true a hundred and fifty years ago, and it's still true today.

The ideal is to work at a job you love doing, and make enough to live on. Some signs are not driven by money at all and will only work at what fulfils them emotionally. That is certainly true of Pisceans. Others will drive themselves along, like Capricorn, at work they don't particularly like, but that makes enough money to get the material things that compensate.

Understanding yourself and finding work that suits you is the ideal compromise. It's not as difficult as you think. Think back to any activity you were engaged in when you felt very happy and content. Or think back to a day when you felt very happy. What were you doing on that day? Was it acting in a play? Was it cooking a meal? Was it on a sports field? Was it, maybe, helping a friend solve a problem? That activity is probably your perfect job. Maybe you chose all the right decorations for your home and did a really good job on the house with the materials you had. That could be your perfect job.

You don't have to be limited by age, sex or what you trained for. Neither do you have to be limited by other people's ideas about who or what you are.

Some women are really inventive. They make their career in the home. One client I had for years kept on her job in the bank after she married and had her three children. Gradually the huge cost of child care wore down their joint finances until she had to honestly ask herself what she was contributing to the family budget, after deducting costs for child care from her wages. It was precious little and, she figured, not worth the time she spent away from the home she loved, and the children she adored and missed.

The crunch came for her when the child-minder told her that her youngest had taken his first baby step that day, and she hadn't been there to see it. In our discussion, she said she loved minding her children, doing the housework, and cooking.

She decided to put her bank career on hold for a few years, and turn her home into a business. She was a true Taurean woman, an earth mother, a good practical soul. She reckoned that by questioning every penny of expenditure and making home-made food, she could save a lot on the food bill alone. She didn't like half a dozen different spray cleaners for her home when one product and a lot of elbow grease would do the same job for a fraction of the cost.

Her home and kitchen became her challenge. She dropped some of her fussy Taurean standards and did a wash twice a week. She grew herbs in pots on the kitchen window sill.

She looked at every item of expenditure and asked herself could she make it, bake it, do without it. I went for meals in her house and absolutely loved her home cooking that she was justifiably proud of, even if the home-made jam did run all over the place. She was happy and contented, and so were her children. They weren't massively better off financially, but she had managed to make enough savings in the home to not miss her wages. She was so happy and content that it more than compensated for her very small financial loss.

Another client lost her factory job, and being untrained for anything else, found herself in competition with scores of younger women of all nationalities for fewer and fewer jobs, but being a Gemini, she wasn't going to give up. She was a talker, a good one, and thought sales might suit her. Age was against her. Still she didn't give up, and approached the owners of an apartment complex to offer them the services of her firm, as cleaners of the entrance, stairs, lifts and landing, the glass and doorways. She calculated the length of time it would take and worked out a reasonable hourly rate. She talked her way into the job, not revealing at that stage that the 'firm' consisted of herself alone. Roping in her sister-in-law as a working partner, the two women set to work. Within two years, their old Ford Fiesta was traded in for a new van and they had to employ two other women to manage the seven apartment complexes they now cleaned.

Work at something you are good at and enjoy doing. Whether it's writing a novel, singing in the local pub, doing accounts for people, or helping children and adults with literacy problems. It's easier to be self-employed than you think.

Not every sign likes the responsibility of being self-employed, or can handle the insecurity of it. Virgoans don't like the unknown or uncertainty, and would far rather be an employee.

Think about what you are good at and enjoy doing, then see if there is any demand out there for what you do. It's a recipe for a happier life.

Find Out If Money Is Coming Into Your Life

Take an ordinary deck of playing cards and remove the Jokers and all the Twos, Threes, Fours, Fives and Sixes. Put them to one side, as you won't be using them at all.

Shuffle the remaining cards as you think of your question. That question may be about the possibility of money coming into your life soon. When you feel you have shuffled enough, put the cards face down on the table before you and cut them once. Now you are looking at two piles of cards in front of you. Turn each pile over and look at the card on top of each pile. If the Nine of Hearts appears, that is a definite yes, there is money and it will come soon.

Gather up the cards and shuffle again. Now put them face down on the table in front of you and spread them out. Take any six cards out and lay them in a line face up before you. If you are lucky enough to draw four Tens, that is a definite sign that a large sum of money is coming into your life very soon. If you have three Tens and one or two Jacks, that's an indication that you are about to win some money. If the Nine of Hearts appears in your six card line up, then your financial affairs will work out to your satisfaction.

If the Seven and Ten of Spades appear, prepare to meet a big bill coming in. It's not a sign of financial disaster; it is a warning to prepare yourself.

Suppose you are wondering whether to sign a contract, and you shuffle the cards to check on whether or not it is going to work out; if you turn over the Nine of Hearts, that is an excellent omen. The combination of cards signifying a contract are the Ace of Spades and the Ace of Clubs together. The cards right beside those two cards will tell you whether or not the contract is likely to be successful. If you get the Nine of Hearts, that's a brilliant sign. It means go ahead and sign, or that you will get the contract, or that whatever the contract is about will bring success for you. More specifically, if you are wondering if that house or apartment you are after is right for you, or, even, that you are going to get it, then you need to see the Seven of Clubs cut beside, or between, the Ace of Clubs and the Ace of Spades. Those are, specifically, the cards meaning a property contract. It's in the offing, it's being prepared or it's actually ready for signature. The important bit here is to look at the cards closest to that combination. If the Eight of Spades is cut beside them, then either the contract will fall through, or you should definitely not sign, as failure will be the result.

If you are applying for a job and shuffle and draw out six cards, you are looking for a Seven and Eight of Clubs together. That means you will definitely get an interview, and that interview will be soon.

If it's a promotion you're after, or want to know if you are going to pass an exam (it's the same cards for both), then you will want to see the Eight and Nine of Clubs in your six card spread. The Nine of Hearts does just as well. It is the wish card; the highest card in the pack.

Suppose you are wondering if that insurance claim you have put in will succeed; then you need you know if the business will end up and be settled in court, or if it will be settled outside of court. Again, draw out six cards. Three Sevens in a row show that the matter will be resolved in the court room. The Nine of Hearts shows a successful outcome. Two, or even three, Tens show that it will be to your financial advantage.

A person wanting to know the outcome of a separation or divorce is in a more complicated position. Apart from the emotions involved, there is also a matter of justice. Some women feel that they have a rightful entitlement to the house on which they continued to pay the mortgage for the past ten or so years after the partner left. Those women might also have reared their children with no financial help, or very little at any rate, from the ex-partner. They may, when separating, feel that they have a just right to the house. But on the deed of ownership is the name of the ex-partner, and it's very hard for them to accept that the judge in court has to act on what is legally written on that house deed. That he may be still legally entitled to his share doesn't seem right or just, but that legal entitlement still exists.

Solicitors aren't hard or harsh, but they don't have the woman's emotional involvement with the separation; they can only advise on how the law stands.

Some signs of the zodiac are better at negotiating with a difficult or greedy ex, and, of course, it depends on his birth sign too. Maybe he will be prepared to act justly, maybe he won't. It really helps to look at your ex's sign of the zodiac and see if he will act with heart, and therefore act fairly, or if he just wants as much money as he can lay his hands on. The cards are also really helpful in this respect.

If you draw Diamonds, you can tell that he is being secretive and uncommunicative, and is probably not telling his solicitor everything either. It's not the end of the world; there is still room for negotiation, but you have to be very diplomatic to ferret out the truth or what his intentions are. If you draw mainly Club cards then he is all about money, but is prepared to talk about it. Mainly Spade cards tell you that he is so caught up in bitterness, emotional hurt, and a desire to hurt you, that he won't think or act rationally. Mainly Heart cards are reassuring, as they are telling you that if you are prepared to sit down and negotiate as much of the business of breaking up as possible, together, as a couple, then neither of you will cause your solicitors too much time or trouble because you will each be able to present a package on which both of you have agreed. It also means that your individual bills will be less, so that there is more of the joint money left to be divided up.

Dream Your Way To A Fortune

I've always been fascinated by dreams; that private place inside your own world that works out all your problems for you, tells you what the problems are and also hands you on a plate, or pillow, the right solutions. Dreams are direct messages from your subconscious mind, working out problems, reassuring you, helping you. If you start to analyse your dreams you will acquire a very valuable tool in helping to analyse the most important issues in your life right now, and, more importantly, find solutions.

Dreams telling you that you need to clean up your financial act are varied and surprising. If you dream that you have problems with your teeth, this is usually a warning that problems are coming in your financial life. If your teeth are aching in the dream then you need to take a look at your finances as they are causing difficulties. Stop spending and start putting by. If your teeth were very loose or actually fell out that is a clear warning of a very large bill on its way to you. It's best to plan a completely different way of handling your finances. Another adverse dream is of finding money or a purse or handbag full of money. This means that you'll be paying out soon and it might be a headache.

On the contrary, any dreams of paying money out is always a sign of money coming in. You might dream of finding an empty purse or handbag. In the dream you might be disappointed, but in waking life it means that money is on the way to you. I don't know why your subconscious plays reverse psychology games, but that is my experience of dreams and the perceived wisdom of dream interpretation.

Are you wondering what dreams predict a win? Of course you are, and it's only natural. You might be horrified in a dream to see hair on some unusual part of your body, say on your neck or stomach, and I don't mean a fine covering of normal body hair but real growth. Be happy. That's a sign that money is on the way to you.

Eating ice-cream in a dream is another sign that unexpected money is coming to you. If you saw mint growing in your dream or tasted it or smelt it, that's another very good money sign.

Dreams of bright colours always raise your spirits and make you feel very good on waking up. So they should, as they are a forerunner of huge financial success. If the predominant colour was a clear and vibrant blue you can be certain that a very large sum of money is coming to you right out of the blue.

Feeding pigeons in your dream is a sign of some bill or other demand for money, one that you had either forgotten or hadn't anticipated — better start putting a bit of money to one side.

Eating pork, or seeing it cooked, or serving it to others is a dream sign that money is approaching.

The Secrets Of Money Luck

———◆———

Pigeons have always been associated with financial luck. If a pigeon landed on your doorstep, you can be sure that he is bringing financial luck into your life. If the pigeon actually walked over the threshold and into the hallway, or kitchen, that's a sure sign that money is on the way. Be nice to pigeons, they're good birds to have around.

If your left palm itches you can be certain that money is on its way to you. If you are around a lotto ticket office, or near a place to buy Prize Bonds and buy when your left palm itches, you can be certain of being very lucky.

Some people say that it's unlucky to wish for money. I think that's ridiculous — why not wish for money? Money is important, very important. Ask anyone who is on a low income or who has been faced with huge financial problems where the bad luck lies. They will tell you it is not having money that is bad luck, and nothing to do with the very natural wish to have enough to keep you happy.

According to the Chinese practice of Feng Shui (arranging your home and furniture in such a way as to bring happiness and harmony into your life) you should get three medallions with a hole through each, or three rings, and thread a red ribbon or piece of twine through them, to hold the three together. You should then place them in the left hand corner of each room. That protects finances and promises an increase in financial fortunes. Every little practice helps, I believe.

People who constantly say that they will never win have given that message to themselves and to the universe. Yet some people do seem luckier than others. The sign of Pisceans might seem dreamily muddled at times, yet, especially from thirty-eight onwards I have noticed they tend to attract a lot of money into their lives. Pisceans often win money.

There are lucky numbers associated with each sign of the zodiac. These numbers could be used in competitions, house numbers, phone numbers or car numbers. They will increase your chance of financial luck:

ARIES	1, 5, 7
TAURUS	2, 6, 14
GEMINI	3, 8, 19
CANCER	9, 18, 27
LEO	9, 21, 35
VIRGO	22, 29, 36
LIBRA	8, 19, 40
SCORPIO	2, 5, 42
SAGITTARIUS	11, 26, 41
CAPRICORN	18, 29, 37
AQUARIUS	4, 6, 27
PISCES	5, 18, 27

REVEAL THE SECRETS OF YOUR BIRTH NUMBER

———

I t's very easy to get your birth number. Just write down the day and month of your birth and add it across the page.

Here's how: 26th November is 26/11. Add across the page, adding the 2 onto the 6, making 8. Then add 1, giving you 9. Then add the other 1, giving a score of 10. You have ended up with 10. Now add the two together, that's 1 added on to 0, or 1+0 = 1.

14th May is 14/5. Add these numbers across the page, and again you end up with 10. Add the 1 onto the 0 and you end up with 1+0 = 1.

1st January is 1/1, so add 1+1 and you get a birth number of 2.

5th of November is 5/11. Add 5 onto 1 to make 6, add on the other 1, and that makes a birth number of 7.

The birth numbers go from 1 to 9. The lower numbers are the more outgoing and sociable while the higher numbers 7, 8 and 9, are more solitary and spiritual.

Birth Number 1
You are creative, energetic and ambitious. You'll try out new things as you are keen to learn and explore new ideas. You've got a strong personality and everyone notices you. You've got your own individual style

— others may copy you. But you can be very good at looking after number one and sometimes don't like people getting too close to you. The dangers are that you might get a bit withdrawn and sorry for yourself at times. Walking and swimming are excellent therapies for you in a down mood.

You need a strong minded, independent partner, but you can survive quite happily on your own.

You like creative work; money isn't your driver. You do what you do because you enjoy it. You may need someone to advise you financially, as this is your weak point.

Birth Number 2

A sensitive and very intuitive person. You like caring for others and you make an excellent listener. You think carefully about decisions and usually make the right decisions for you and those you care for. Sharing is your favourite pastime. You share your emotions, your time, your home even. You enjoy helping others and are a loving and stable influence in the lives of those around you.

On a bad day you can be touchy and moody and if anyone says a cross word you can sulk for hours. You like your advice being taken and if it's rejected you react strongly. You are very cautious and sometimes slow to act.

You're a healthy person who enjoys quality food, plenty of sleep and lovely mood music.

You need a partner who is as warm and loving as you are. You might both share an interest in psychology, therapy and alternative medicine, and even a partner to share your chosen career, maybe in a caring profession like counselling. Ideally your chosen partner would be a good financial balancer as you have a tendency to hoard up money as though you secretly fear poverty.

Birth Number 3

You are a number of physical and emotional energy with a great sense of humour and a very easy-going nature. All sorts of people are attracted to you because you give them a sense of well-being. You show them how to take life in their stride, cope with its difficulties and get on with it.

Secretly you can sometimes be very critical of yourself and feel unable to get yourself organised. It's a wonder if you can actually find things easily around the home as you can be messy, untidy and disorganised.

Birth number 3 is most associated with health and medicine. Your chief health asset is your relaxed attitude to life. You deal well with stress and cleverly avoid stressful situations. You are also attracted to careers in the health service. If you are interested in sales, and with birth number 3 you are good at sales, it may be a health product. You bring energy and enthusiasm to everything you do.

Your partner is your chief source of happiness and well-being. In love you commit easily and naturally. You are attracted to artistic, creative types. Together you make a good financial combination and are usually lucky all your adult life. Money is attracted to you.

Birth Number 4
In early life things are often hard for you. You have the knack, if confronted with choice, of choosing the harder of the two roads open to you. In the second half of your life things go into reverse and all of life's goodies flow into your life — love, money, attractive looks and good health. You like a structured routine. You had to make yourself, home and family secure. Your many friends like, admire and depend on you.

Maybe you need to take time out of your hard-working routine, just for you. You need time to relax, and you need to accept the fact that you are entitled once in a while to do absolutely nothing and re-charge the batteries.

You certainly work at your relationship. You want it warm, safe, steady and secure. That's what you give and that's what you want and need in return.

Book-keeping or accountancy are good careers for you. You also enjoy housekeeping, gardening and cooking. Busy and active, you thrive.

As you work so hard for your money you aren't prepared to risk it. If you have spare money to invest, put it into bricks and mortar, as property always seems the most sensible proposition to you.

Birth Number 5
You are the passionate flirt of the birth numbers. You like life to move fast and with loads of variety. Every day is a new adventure to you. You dislike routine and all the different aspects of your busy life fascinate you. Other people are drawn to you, to your charm, your

quick wit and inventive personality. They never quite know what to expect as you're pretty changeable.

You'll travel at every available opportunity, as there is a restlessness about you. You might charge out of a job or relationship without giving it too much thought. Your stormy moods and outbursts are legendary.

You're not often found suffering ill-health. You have a healthy zest for life and like a partner who shares this with you.

You make a great teacher, salesperson, travel guide or writer. You like money and it likes you, and one way or another you usually end up with a lot of it, and hopefully a partner wise enough to make sure you hang on to it.

Birth Number 6

This is one of the really stable numbers. Home and property are very important to you. On a property hunt you have the knack of finding the right one at your price. Once your dream home is yours you'll fill it with perfectly chosen furniture and furnishings.

Your take great care of your partner and children but because you sometimes allow yourself to become everyone's slave you can get resentful about being taken for granted. Stop brooding and take positive action. You are health and diet conscious and opt for organic whenever you can. If you do go on an occasional food binge it really isn't as harmful as you think so try not to punish yourself.

You like being in a relationship and to create a romantic atmosphere for you and your partner.

Commitment is second nature to you.

You like to train for a career that you can turn into a business. You've got an excellent head for business and are prepared to work hard. That money you earn is ploughed back into the home so that the family can share the fruits of your successful labour.

Birth Number 7

You are the most likely number to be psychic, and if not psychic, at least extremely intuitive. You are the perfect bridge between the world of commerce and the more sensitive world of the telepathic personality. Your excellent manners and worldly knowledge earn you a lot of respect and popularity. You are a deep thinker. Sometimes this deep thought is carried a bit too far so that you feel isolated from other people as you dwell in your own thoughts.

Yoga and meditation are good practices for you, as they help keep your active mind and healthy body in balance.

In relationships you are always searching for a soul mate and won't commit until you feel certain that your partner is right for you. When you do, your relationship is for keeps.

You make a gifted and inspired teacher, but you've got artistic and creative abilities too, and photography might be a career or even a great hobby for you.

You are the birth number most likely to make or win a fortune.

Birth Number 8

You think about things a lot and often find that what you think about, dream about and wish for actually comes true. You have masses of natural energy, creative brains and the capacity and willingness to work very hard. You are a success story. When people say you are lucky they don't realise just how much sheer hard work you have to put in to attain your achievements. You like making money and spending it on luxury items. If the money runs out you re-adapt, re-organise and make some more.

Other people don't have your capacity for fast and deep thought, or your organisational skills. You may sometimes demand more of them, thinking of them as lazy or poorly motivated because they can't achieve what you can. What seems easy to you is beyond most other people's capacity. You'll have to allow for that. Try to get your own way without being bossy or argumentative. You don't need to be.

You have a fantastic constitution but because of over work you sometimes run out of energy and need to get away from work and out into the fresh air. Watching a sport like horse racing or a match might be ideal. Ideally, go with your partner, as chances are the partner needs to be dragged away from work too as you are attracted to equally independent and powerful people.

There isn't anything you couldn't tackle career wise. You could run a recruitment agency or an industrial cleaning firm. The law or accountancy would also appeal. As a personal secretary to a business tycoon or head of a large corporation, you would be in your element.

Fortunately you have a very healthy respect for the money you make and manage to hold onto most of it.

Birth Number 9

This is an unusual number and belongs to unusual people. You are most likely to rise to the top of a chosen profession or career. You have great leadership qualities and are capable of deeply spiritual thought. You make wise judgements and like to see justice done. You might even fight for justice. You like to see change for the better. You have the power to influence people and their lives. You would make a good teacher, trainer, doctor or nurse.

You need to stop criticising yourself and stop preaching at people. You can convince them in more positive ways. You like approval but there are times when you can be very secretive. You need to share knowledge and information much more.

Health-wise, you make sure to stay in good shape and practice relaxation techniques. You relax best with your partner. You can be unexpectedly romantic and are attracted to artistic and musical types.

Money is attracted to you, and the more you give to charity the more money comes flowing your way. You are quite likely to end up with a fortune. Winner is stamped all over you.

Find That Perfect Job

———◆———

One of the signs that really hates routine is PISCES. Anything that has a rigid nine to five routine is definitely not for them. Neither can they stomach a boss who is a stickler for time. Typically Pisceans will be regularly late for work. The excuse is always wonderful. This is one of the most creative signs of the zodiac and each excuse for being late on that particular morning sounds like the plot of a very good film. A wise boss of the Piscean employee will be able to look beyond the constant lateness and admit that their Piscean employee brings fun, hard work and charm to the workplace. It's always a happier place to be with the Piscean around.

Co-workers and customers love the Piscean, because they inspire real affection in people, promote harmony in the work place and are the peacemakers in many situations. They don't moan if there is a sudden rush of work ten minutes before knocking off time either. Instead, they pitch in without complaining and do what has to be done. There is a sense of loyalty about them that is quite inspirational. They are kind and giving and are often taken advantage of by the boss who is unscrupulous enough to still bear a grudge at five o'clock because Pisces scrambled in a bit late that morning.

Pisces learns by watching other people. Put Pisces into a kitchen and observe them watching the chef at work. They are eager to try out something themselves and if given gentle encouragement and praise they learn cooking skills very quickly. As confidence grows they begin to experiment, their creative mind improving on dishes intuitively. Put that Piscean into a classroom and instruct them on exactly the same dish and watch the eyes glaze over and the mind switch off.

Pisces is a water sign with the fish as its symbol. A lot of Pisceans have work that is somehow linked to both. If not work, then maybe the hobby has that link. Ideally Pisceans should turn their favourite hobby into their occupation.

A Piscean career could be in fish, either farming it, cooking it, selling it, marketing it, advertising it or painting it. Ideally, working in a seafood restaurant that sells good wine would be a Piscean heaven. Wine, or any alcohol for that matter is very attractive to Pisceans. The bar trade and hotel business has a huge number of Piscean employees and most Pisceans have at some point or other in their lives worked in a food or drink outlet.

The Piscean student taking on some bar or restaurant work to make money has a fabulous time. They enjoy what they do, learn a lot and make friends, often life-long ones in such a setting. They bring the skills learned in a part-time job home, and keep them for life.

But Pisces is also drawn to other liquids like water, oil, dyes (Pisceans dye their hair from a young age, more often and more bizarrely than any other sign) and chemicals and paints. They could work in any capacity with those materials.

As a swimming coach or instructor Pisces is very much at home. Just occasionally, Pisces has a phobia about water and can't and won't go near it. Then, the idea of swimming is a nightmare. But most Pisceans love the water and have been typical water babies. In fact, having a shower is a favourite Piscean occupation, but one can't really make a living out of that. With their great inter-personal skills, Pisceans make wonderful swimming teachers for nervous first-timers of any age. However clumsy and awkward they are in day to day life, just put them into the water and watch them glide gracefully off. Swimming is also a great therapy for depressed Pisceans. Overwork sometimes makes them moody and cross and a long swim cheers them up.

Working either as an artist or interior designer, Pisces incorporates water, fish and plants into many themes. The water colours of blue, grey and aquamarine feature very prominently. Working for an employer or maybe self-employed as a painter and decorator, Pisces shows a real flair and creative imagination as well as skill and hard work.

The part of the body associated with the sign of Pisces is the feet. So working in, or even owning a shoe shop is a good area. I am emphasising self-employment a lot because once Pisces has brought up the confidence levels, they are well adapted to working for themselves. They have a good business instinct and money is attracted to Pisces. Unfortunately Pisces is attracted and sometimes addicted to spending money. Pisceans looking to any medical profession — and Pisces is associated with medicine — chiropody is a satisfying career. It also lends itself to self-employment. Piscean chiropodists, apart from being skilled and gentle, also show great counselling skills. Although medicine is associated with Pisces, they don't necessarily make good counsellors, particularly not to their friends as they tend to get bored and impatient with a catalogue of moans and groans. Yet with a patient sitting in the chiropody chair, the Piscean practitioner has the knack of drawing the patient out, letting them talk, listening with courteous attention and encouraging them to off-load a lot of grievances and worries.

Where Pisces shines is in the area of caring for patients with whom they can develop a long term relationship; say with any form of disability, either mental or physical. They work well with children but better with adults who are maybe in a long-term care situation. To see a Piscean working with an elderly person is actually very moving. I remember watching a young Piscean nurse relating to an elderly man in a hospital ward for long-term elderly patients. She chatted with him, laughed with him and soon was going through his photographs looking at them with real curiosity and interest. Soon he was telling her about his life, his recollections and his childhood. They were stories from another age, a forgotten one, but brought to vivid and poignant life by that girl's ability to draw the old man out. She created a warm and patient space for him, and gave him her time. I felt the power and charm of the Piscean spirit at work.

Many Pisceans are drawn to glamorous work. They like being in boutiques, trendy clothes shops, anywhere where individual fashion is made, bought or sold. Most Pisceans aren't tall enough for modelling which is a pity because Pisceans have a special relationship with clothes and fashion. Even when the Piscean puts on weight in later life and can't wear the slender flowing lines that suit them so well they don't lose their interest in fashion and make inspired advisors for younger people. If you want a great and sympathetic wedding organiser, grab a Piscean. As a career in organising events, especially weddings or fashion events, Pisces is second to none.

A lot of Pisceans are drawn to the theatre. It might be an involvement with local amateur dramatics, or to the professional theatre. It might be in any capacity, cleaning, selling tickets or coffee, acting, doing make-up, or whatever. If it's designing or making clothes, then Pisces is very much in the right place. Pisces puts in hours and hours of hard and creative work cheerfully, without fuss and definitely not for money.

Pisces is not driven by money. Pisces is driven by a need to enjoy what they do, to get satisfaction from it. For that reason a lot of Pisceans seem to find themselves in low paid work or even unpaid charity work. Others are drawn to music and often work for years writing and singing songs for little or no money. Others might work in a music shop.

If you get a home-made card for Christmas or your birthday, I'll bet it comes from a Piscean. And talking of betting, Pisceans are drawn to gambling and might find themselves working in a betting shop, or the betting shop on the grand scale, the bank or stock exchange.

High status jobs don't hold much attraction for them though. Essentially it's people that the Piscean is drawn to, people who impress them, like original or creative thinkers or people who are psychic, sensitive or intuitive, or maybe very glamorous. They avoid people who are interested only in money, or status, or who are aggressive and demanding.

Pisceans also need to avoid jobs that are physically demanding, or where people tend to work to the clock or a set routine, such as in a factory or office. That is a recipe for depression and anxiety.

Pisceans also make great religious or spiritual workers. They are the cheerful and uncomplaining light in others' lives.

SAGITTARIUS is one sign that is very difficult to pin down in early life. They abound with a restless energy and never seem to stop talking. They appear friendly but undisciplined and it seems hard to categorise them enough to slot them easily into one career or another. They spend money with little thought to tomorrow and saving money never seems to occur to them. Parents often think their Sagittarian off-spring will have a good career in sport. But whereas the Sagittarian youngster will have an enthusiasm for all sports they won't necessarily have the discipline for training and the commitment to care too deeply about winning each and every time. Older people may look at them and listen to their non-stop talk and think that they might make a very good teacher, then close observation reveals that they have the tendency to start lots of learning programmes but often stop or back out, before something is finished. The wild enthusiasm they showed at the beginning of the month has quite disappeared by the end of the month. They show promise in lots of areas but often don't have sufficient interest in a specific area to work at it steadily and consistently.

It is quite possible that the typical Sagittarian has had four or five distinctly different and apparently quite unrelated careers under their belt by the time they are thirty-five. Closer examination will reveal that there are clear links between these apparently unrelated areas.

Sagittarius works with the mind, has ideas and is often idealistic. It is also a creative mind, not necessarily inventive. Sagittarians won't invent a better electric kettle, or design a car that will perform better and look more stylish than the last model. But they will pursue an 'ideas' career. They are among the finest brains in the whole zodiac. Combine those oratorical gifts, their capacity to talk well, use that accurate memory with the capacity to absorb huge amounts of new knowledge very quickly, and have a very impressive aura and you have the perfect barrister. Sagittarians are drawn to the law. They aren't necessarily always law-abiding, they are impatient of convention and won't have too much respect for traditional ideas and practices, but they find the law fascinating. An ideal hobby for them is to go into the public gallery in the court room and watch all the mini-dramas being played out in real life. They like reading accounts of trials and are intrigued by the careers of great criminals or great judges.

They enjoy learning and never lose their pleasure in discovering some new facts. Some Sagittarians I know make a hobby out of reading the statistic books drawn up after the census has been taken. They speculate on and wonder at facts about more people taking holidays on the Costa del Sol, or that the second child in the family is more accident prone than the first or third child. What they are able to do is to hold all these apparently unrelated facts and bits of knowledge in their heads and to make connected sense of them.

The centaur, half-horse, half human is the symbol of Sagittarius and many Sagittarians are drawn to working with horses, watching them race, betting on the outcome of the race, photographing horses, loving the beauty and nobility of the horse. Adult Sagittarians are drawn to joining a horse-owning syndicate. They might only have very little money to contribute to a very large syndicate, but they absolutely revel in it. The way the Sagittarian admires and respects the courage and competitive nature of the horse tells observers a great deal about the Sagittarian personality and their attitude to work and life. It truly is not the winning that inspires Sagittarius but the manner in which the competition is handled.

Many Sagittarians get drawn into local politics because they feel strongly about a particular issue. They may see something that is either unfair or needs changing and set out to achieve that single issue. If they get drawn into the social aspect of the political group they might stay on. Sagittarians are attracted to politics; again it's the ideas and the issues, rather than the nitty-gritty day to day workings of political life, that attract them. Most Sagittarians are disillusioned by the underhandedness, false promises and conniving they believe takes place in political life. They like justice and will champion the underdog. They are inspired by tales of great leaders, revolutionaries and noble causes.

They excel in writing about politicians, criticising them, even making jokes about them and their activities. Any career in journalism is attractive to Sagittarians. They have as good written skills as verbal ones. They might write about or comment on sport, especially horse racing with as much ease and competence as they write about and broadcast about the events in the council chamber. But they combine wit, humour and sarcasm and if their poetical idealism is offended they viciously satirise phoney or pompous councillors or politicians.

Sagittarians have great comic skills and can turn the most sombre or sad subject into an hilarious joke whilst giving some very wise insights into even the most painful subjects. Scottish comedian and great Sagittarian, Billy Connolly is probably the best example of this.

Sagittarians make good teachers or instructors especially as they get older. They are more patient and have more reasonable expectations of trainees or students. But if the Sagittarian won't take the time and trouble and develop the staying power to actually focus for long enough to get a qualification, they often end up in work that under-uses their brain and intelligence and they get bored. Boredom and routine are the great Sagittarian killers.

Typically the Sagittarian will let all the housework, washing, ironing and tidying mount up until everything is in one almighty muddle. They then wake one morning with a huge amount of energy, and tear through everything from morning until night, all the time making resolutions that things will never get into this state again. They vow that they are going, from now on, to stick to a regular cleaning and tidying routine. They put the new plan and resolution into place and it might even last a whole week.

They plan diets and menus and budget carefully; their intentions are truly excellent, but are soon abandoned. But most Sagittarians acquire wisdom and discipline with age. It's because they never lose the capacity to learn.

Never put a Sagittarian on an assembly line, as fiddly, repetitive, detailed work is completely beyond them. They won't be attentive enough and will make mistakes. They probably won't care about or take responsibility for the mistakes.

What they do like to do is pass on the knowledge they have to others, so that people can benefit from it. That is why you need to motivate and impose some gentle discipline on Sagittarian teenagers to complete a course of study so that they can apply their knowledge in teaching, medicine, the law or journalism. These areas attract them, inspire them and draw out all that is best in their personality.

Being chatty and liking to communicate with others and find out how they think and live, makes Sagittarius a great linguist. They pick up languages very easily, especially if they make regular trips to the countries where they can practise their language skills. They like tour guiding, translating and working in the travel trade. Travel is as natural and necessary to Sagittarians as breathing. They love holidaying, or if young, putting a pack on the back and heading off for distant lands and strange cultures. Many Sagittarians emigrate very successfully because, apart from the excitement of re-locating, they adapt very well and happily to other cultures.

Little Sagittarians absolutely love libraries, museums and art galleries. As long as they can move around a lot, and aren't required to keep completely quiet, they'll spend hours in the library. Books attract them. Editing, books, selling them and publishing them are all great Sagittarian careers. Check out that man or woman on the corner of the street selling the newspapers or magazines, it's most likely a Sagittarian. Best of all Sagittarius is in heaven as a writer. The 'ideas' mind, the interest in people, and wide ranging knowledge all fuse together in creating the novel. Funnily enough, the patience and discipline so often missing when applied to other careers is very evident when Sagittarius sits down to write a novel.

Most people will say that they have a book in them and that people should read about their lives. What they mean is that they believe the average reader really wants to sit down and be riveted by the account of someone else's breakdown, marriage failure, six abortions, drug habit and begging in the street for scraps of food. In Sagittarian hands, such an account would have humour, wit and balance. It's those ingredients that Sagittarius brings to the table of life that makes this such an attractive sign.

Sagittarius is often drawn to religious life in some form or another. It may be taking vows, or working in a religious bookshop, being a priest's housekeeper or singing in a choir. Many Sagittarians, whether religious or not, are attracted to religious monuments, sites or events. They may even like the idea of going on a spiritual retreat from time to time as a way of clearing the mind and finding the spiritual nourishment and refreshment essential to the Sagittarian spirit.

A lot of Sagittarians prefer to work out of doors. They don't like being confined. Driving or even being a driving instructor has appeal. So does long distance haulage work, as long distance driving means that the driver can have a mobile phone, a good radio, and meet friends at all the stopping points.

Sagittarians avoid people who take life too seriously and don't believe that somewhere out there, there is a dash of magic or a guardian angel.

TAURUS is a solid, respectable sign. If you're an employer and you get your hands on a Taurean employee, treasure the gift you have been given. You'll never get a better worker or one more loyal to you. The Taurean employee will actually volunteer for the difficult jobs. They enjoy solving problems and getting things right. I've always thought of Taurus as having the brain of a farmer and the heart and soul of an artist. Artistic ability is in abundance in this sign and if the timing is right, Taurus will abandon that sensible career in the bank and take up interior design or fine art. Being businesslike, Taurus knows how to turn that artistic hobby into a sound business proposition.

Taureans are born with many gifts. One of them is the gift of being able to bargain. Trying to buy a house from a Taurean is quite like trying to play poker against the most hardened gambler in Las Vegas. Taurus gives nothing away, has the price fixed, has read the buyer accurately and knows before the buyer speaks just how much they are prepared to pay.

For some reason, probably because they are innately model citizens, Taureans are drawn to large bureaucratic institutions. They prefer the safety and rules of the big institution to other forms of business. Yet they run up against all sorts of problems in such institutions. Taurus will play by the rules, yet when they find other employees cutting corners, cheating, or being promoted unfairly it brings out their anger. If you ever hear a Taurean co-worker saying that something is not fair, run for cover because that rare but legendary Taurean temper is about to explode. They go on a moral rampage that is the equivalent of Jesus turning over the tables of the money lenders in the temple. Taurus won't rest until justice has been done.

Taurus is a very realistic sign. You want money? You work for it. You don't like your job? Change it. Can't change? Get an interesting hobby. No time for a hobby? Put up and shut up.

Although Taurus is drawn to the safety of the large organisation or even government department, administration really isn't their ideal field. They like to see something at the end of the day, and I literally mean see something that is a direct product of their labours. They want to see cooked food, a wall they've constructed, a car they've fixed, a tree they felled and cut into logs. They want to look at the photos they've taken. They need to see something solid and tangible if they are to feel satisfied with their work. Banking, accountancy or financial services aren't enough.

Even the biggest and roughest of Taureans have the gentlest and the most sensitive hands. The touch is healing which is why it is no surprise to find so many Taureans in medicine and alternative or complementary medicine. I recall a Taurean ward sister, grim-faced, steely-eyed and rather abrupt (when Taureans are concentrating they always appear gruff) but she had the soft and caressing touch of an angel and the certainty in her professional judgement that inspired the sick to get well. Physiotherapy is their speciality.

Taureans frown a lot over their work. They concentrate intensely, wanting to get everything right. No sloppy standards here. Even when doing a job they detest, it's going to be done well.

As Taurus is an earth sign, working out of doors with plants, flowers, vegetables or even farming is an attractive career. I have already mentioned medicine and nursing, and the beauty business is also a likely occupation. It gives Taurus a chance to express the artistic side of their natures.

But the business in which Taureans of all ages excel is property; whether it is building property, painting and decorating, gardening and creating artistic features, speculating on property or working as an auctioneer or valuer. Taurean heaven would be finding an old cottage, something cheap and run down, and doing it up on the inside and outside to that famous Taurean high standard. They will then create the right garden and sell it for many times its original value. The piece of perfection created by Taurus' own hands would be the big kick for this sign. But the healthy and hard won profit would come a very close second.

Food is very important to Taureans. They absolutely love the stuff; more the quality than the quantity, so it's entirely natural to find them in work that is close to food. That's either producing it, cooking it, selling it, or marketing it. As well as liking the taste and aroma of food, Taurus also finds the colours very satisfying. The colours of nature are myriad and deeply appreciated by the sensual Taurean nature. Rusts and oranges and the cool neutrals of fine linen are especially appreciated.

Don't take on any work where you have to work to a deadline, Taurus, you'll hate it. Unless your best friend has asked you to design her wedding dress at short notice. But you could look at work where you'd be paid a commission. Apart from selling houses, you might look at selling all the things that go into the house: furniture, fine art, paintings, posters, kitchenware, garden furniture. And talking of garden furniture, you might even try making it yourself. It would be handcrafted, the best, beautifully and artistically finished and would sell for a very healthy profit.

🐏 **ARIES** — Anyone can recognise an Aries from miles off. For starters, they never stop moving. They gesticulate a lot, moving hands and arms when talking. They smile a lot (that smile can turn into a nasty frown and as quickly back to the charming smile). They talk a lot, giving orders, then checking to see that the orders are carried out. That's an Aries problem — they can't delegate anything. They bore easily and move onto something else. They size up a task quickly, give the appropriate orders and watch it through to completion. And dare anyone to question, oppose or countermand the Arian order. Hell to pay! Notice how many times I mentioned those words, 'order' and 'quickly'? Aries are the born leaders of the zodiac. Whenever I hear of a disaster somewhere I'm longing to tell them to send an Aries in, the problem, no matter how large, will be sorted out very quickly and very efficiently. It is not just giving the order, it is knowing what has to be done.

The more Aries has to do, the happier they are. Aries thrives on activity. They seem impulsive — they aren't really, it's just that they know what has to be done and how it has to be done, and then it's done quickly because they don't need to spend time talking about it. Endless meetings and discussions about proposed actions drive Aries mad. They see it as time wasting. But if you do call Aries to a meeting, be on time. They are excellent timekeepers, and they'll probably arrive early for any appointment.

Aries' weak point in work is that they often can't understand how other people feel. If work needed to be halted because a co-worker needed to talk about how they felt about the break-up of their new relationship, or wanted to off-load anxiety about some financial worries, Aries might get irritated. They reason that the emotional situation exists, but it is outside of working hours, it is a fact of that person's life and should, in any case, be saved for discussion in out of work hours. They probably wouldn't actually say that such emotional talk is a waste of time, but they might feel it. An Aries boss with a Pisces employee appears more like an ineffectual dithering half-wit. The woman of action cannot understand the gentle creature of emotion, and vice-versa.

Aries is often better off working alone. The job gets done, quickly and efficiently. Most Arians should seriously consider working for themselves. There is very little that Aries can't do. They can move from being a talented computer worker to making items to be sold on a market stall. Arians are usually very good at business. They enjoy the risk, the constant change, and ceaseless demands on their time.

Astrologically, Arians are the sports people of the zodiac but as most Arians can't be full-time sports people they could look at the next best thing.

Working in a stable, or even running the stable would be a marvellous job. Loads of variety and a sense of achievement are required. Making jewellery, or anything in metal, and selling it, is also a good move. Arians don't like being tied down, preferring to be on the move. Delivering stuff from business to business is a fun and very Arian thing to do. Running a flower business from home and making all the deliveries is also a good option. Making a small business out of collecting lost luggage (once the airport have located it) and re-uniting it with its owner, is another option. Working in a laundry; that involves being on the move and seeing a beautiful end result. Aries likes to see an end result for all their work. Working in the props department in film or in theatre is another job that Aries loves doing.

Writing for the local or regional paper, and being a roving reporter is a superb job for Aries. Arians are also drawn to uniforms and any job involving the wearing of a uniform suits them very well. As a buyer for a store, especially a supermarket, Arians can have all the activity and variety they crave. Landscape gardening, especially doing a quick make-over, is an Aries speciality. Something crazy but wonderful will result.

Aries is a very physical sign and enjoys doing things. Put Aries behind a desk and they are fidgeting and fussing and getting bored and frustrated. They begin to find fault with themselves. They are a very straightforward type and rarely blame anyone else when something goes wrong in their working lives. And they do take corrective action quickly. An employer will find they are great workers, but won't hold onto them for long. Typically, Aries will have sampled five or six different jobs quite early on in life, before deciding on what they want to turn into a career.

If you have an Aries teenager, or you are a young Arian seeming to drift from job to job, don't worry about it because variety is very, very good for you. It helps you sample many new types of work, gives lots of experience, and teaches an awareness about other people. That is a valuable lesson.

Another enterprise Aries might consider is buying junk and working on it until it has become a work of art and selling it on. I have known many Arians who have taken fantastic and improbable risks and come out winning.

Aries works very well in transport of any form. Traffic control in an airport is pretty static, but not to an Arian who understands the vital importance of anything they are doing. Being a taxi-driver is another Aries option. Keeping the world on the move is Aries' mission in life. Aries is rarely bothered by status so this sign is good at turning their hands to just about anything. As an Aries, it's good to work with all sorts of machinery and tools, even weapons.

Keep moving, keep thinking, keep problem solving and Aries, you will keep happy in work.

🐾 AQUARIUS — This is the most difficult sign to categorise. There are as many types of Aquarian as there are signs of the zodiac. They can go from alert and enquiring to outright eccentric. But Aquarians do have amazingly quick wits and a very keen, intelligent brain. Aquarians can be very tough, to the point of cruelty. Aquarians can also be so very vulnerable that they pluck at the heart strings of those around them.

Aquarians can be very humane, kind and caring, but they can also be so self-centred that those who have to work with them wonder if that Aquarian has ever heard a single word spoken to them, or if they could have cared less.

This apparent selfishness comes from the deeply felt need Aquarius has to exercise and express individual thought and freedom. But even the severest critic of an Aquarian has to admit that this sign has a creative genius, an ability to cope with, work with and understand new technology. Aquarius can also see the immense potential of new technology.

Aquarius takes a humane view of mankind. It is a generous sign in accepting human weakness and they make few judgements on other people. If faced with coping with a disaster and many human lives needing to be saved, the cool Aquarian mind swings into action and knows that communication is essential. Rescue personnel would be immediately equipped with a fleet of mobile phones, a command and accountability structure is put into place, and Aquarius has the intuitive skill to put the right people in the right place, then sit back and watch the whole operation in motion. Their feelings are detached, interested only in the procedures. It wouldn't matter to Aquarius whether the people needing help were a group of orphans or prisoners on the run. Both prisoners and orphans appeal to Aquarians. But they are not as fascinating as technology.

I'm guessing that probably half of the key and best employees in information technology are Aquarians.

Anything and everything to do with radio, sound engineering, railways, aviation, electricity, telephone systems, and so on, are Aquarian areas. Music in all its forms is another love of Aquarius. Aquarius relates differently to music than other signs. Music entertains them, intrigues them and excites them.

Aquarians need to understand exactly what they are doing and exactly what is required of them. They need to see in writing exactly what the job brief is. If they are in control before starting, then the Aquarian is happy and confident. Unclear areas and a boss who constantly has changes of mind all conspire to drive Aquarius mad. Sometimes Aquarian behaviour appears completely mad to observers. Yet it is found that there is method in their madness, a method that achieves results.

An ideal job for the non-technical Aquarian is in any type of social work. Many Aquarians have very strong and active humanitarian principles. They burn with a sense of injustice and want to put things right. They will work as a teacher or maybe a social worker because it feels right. It is a contribution to life for the benefit of humanity. Teaching literacy to adults is something Aquarians excel at. Working in a newspaper dedicated to social justice is another area where the Aquarian shines.

Whether Aquarius goes to work in a supermarket, a hospital, a social services department or a factory making music equipment, this sign can recognise instantly how things could be done better and more efficiently. A wise boss will listen and put some if not all of those ideas into action, because they come from an unusual space. It is a mixture of psychic intuition, logical thinking, the ability to understand how processes work and an appreciation of what the end result of the organisation should be.

Watch a worker or even a customer re-arranging things in a shop — that's probably an Aquarian. That visitor who rearranged your kitchen while you were gossiping with other guests was probably an Aquarian. This isn't just a polite way of saying that Aquarians can sometimes be tactless; they are well meaning. There is a loveable quality about Aquarians that shines through at all times.

Because Aquarians are knowledgeable, informed and excellent talkers, they are often put into sales or drift into sales. It's not particularly a strong point as Aquarius is rarely motivated by money. In fact, the naked profit motive revolts Aquarius. The neighbour of an Aquarian was in trouble because the landlord wanted the family out in order to sell the property at a huge profit. The Aquarian woman in question knew that the landlord had inherited the house from his mother. She also knew that her neighbours had been good tenants doing repairs and maintenance on the property for years at their own expense. Their plight touched her heart and offended her Aquarian principles. She gathered all the legal information she needed to mount a campaign against the offending landlord on her neighbours' behalf. As the law was not on her side, she went to the local newspapers and radio station. She also mounted a one-woman-picket at his house. A one woman picket may not sound like a ferocious threat to a money-hungry landlord, but when that woman is an Aquarian, that's a formidable force to be reckoned with. The neighbours did eventually move, but not for the lack of effort on the part of the Aquarian who just had to try to help in some way.

That the Aquarian woman never said anything afterwards shows another side to the work potential of the Aquarian; they can be remarkably discreet. This is astounding given that Aquarians sometimes can't keep quiet about anything. This discretion, along with other remarkable qualities, make Aquarius an ideal candidate for working as a private detective. There are many aspects to private detection work, but work involving security has great appeal to the Aquarian.

An increasing number of Aquarians offer their skills and services to Third World countries. And sometimes in late life the Aquarian woman will down tools and go off to do some charity work, whether it is abroad or at home.

Somehow Aquarius manages to have fun at work. Even the dreariest, most boring and repetitive work is livened up by the presence of the Aquarian. They can joke about anything, don't want to be serious all the time and can, when they choose, cheer people up.

Don't put Aquarians to work with food, or pandering to the whims of the idle rich. It doesn't work. I often wondered if that eccentric hotelier, Basil Fawlty of television fame was an Aquarian. Bet you he was!

CANCER and people go together hand in hand. Cancerians often appear to be loners because they are gentle and self-effacing, and shy away from praise. But Cancerians need people. They need to work with people, a lot of people; they enjoy helping people and caring for them. They focus intently on a person who is off-loading all of their current problems. The very act of listening is helpful. Cancer won't judge and probably, unless directly asked, won't give an opinion. But neither will Cancer ever divulge something they have been told in confidence. Cancerians love all the interaction and gossip that goes on in the workplace, but if they have been told something in confidence, or feel that the stuff they have heard is of a confidential nature, they will never repeat it.

Others feel in very safe hands with a Cancerian. They are the carers of the zodiac. So it is often overlooked, except by a very clever boss, that Cancerians have excellent management skills. They understand their work, and work very hard, often putting in all those extra hours without complaining, but they also understand people.

In management, Cancerians have the knack of pointing out a subordinate's fault without making the person feel demeaned. In fact they encourage that person to try again and be successful. For that reason, Cancerians make superb teachers or trainers. Their sensitive understanding of others and the ability to relate very easily to people is a key factor in their success in teaching and training. They also make great nurses, doctors, psychotherapists and counsellors. The qualities needed in each of those jobs is second nature to Cancerians.

But there is also an ordered and logical mind and very shrewd judgement. Cancerians don't like taking chances: gambling or risking and speculating is not in their nature. If they do go in for buying up and selling on properties, you can be sure it's because they have identified a need in the market and only buy when they can be sure of selling on. Profit is not what drives a Cancerian. Although many opt for the safe and secure jobs in offices, administration, bookkeeping and accountancy, they always seek the human contact element of their work. Office work would need to be in a hospital, health board or social services setting. Cancerians need to feel that their work is directed towards helping other people.

Ideally the Cancerian woman likes to work from home. She enjoys looking after her husband, children, parents and parents-in-law. If she has to work outside the home it must be the right sort of job for her, otherwise she becomes really unhappy. She prefers to be at home caring for her brood.

More than any other sign, Cancerians become aware that they aren't happy at work. Money must be earned, the mortgage or rent has to be paid, the children must be fed, or if the Cancerian lives alone, which is rare for Cancerians, a decent lifestyle has to be maintained. Cancer isn't driven by money and they are not in the least impressed by others' displays of wealth. Cancer is always a realistic sign. If one needs money, go out and earn it. But if Cancer finds that they feel reluctance to go to work, gets stomach pains, begin to increase around the waistline, or gets frequent headaches, the first need is to stop self-blame and look at the nature of the work. Examine it carefully and ask a number of key questions.

- Did someone at school suggest a career path?
- Was there a logical progression from one examination to another?
- Did it fit in with parental wishes and approval that a particular career was followed?

Because most Cancerians are hard-working and successful students, it is supposed, naturally enough, that an academic career is the right one for them. Also because Cancerians have the ability to sit still for hours focusing on studies, it is assumed that they will be quite happy to sit at a desk for hours ploughing through accounts, bookkeeping or doing administrative work. It might be fine for a while. But if Cancer becomes dissatisfied or even depressed by work, it is because there is something wrong with the work and nothing wrong with the Cancerian. In fact, nature is doing something very right. Nature, instinct, intuition is screeching at the hard-working, conscientious Cancerian to get out of that job now.

If there are absolutely no training opportunities or caring work in the local area then Cancer should begin a course of home study, or convert a room in the house and set up a creche. This is satisfying and reasonably well-paid work. Maybe look at the kitchen and make, bake or do without until food expenses are at a minimum, because Cancer is a thrifty and brilliant cook. I won't heap too much cooking praise on Cancerians because they shy away from praise like a vegetarian avoids meat. But Cancerians are brilliant and simple cooks.

Ideally Cancer should be counselling. The most brilliant and inspired counsellors come from the signs of Cancer and Scorpio, with Pisces a close third. After training Cancer could turn the counselling skills into a business and work from home. Cancerians draw people to them to confide problems, have a good gossip and laugh with.

That Cancerian sense of humour is a tremendous asset in the workplace. Somehow the presence of Cancer makes the day seem easier.

Cancer often ends up the wealthiest sign of the zodiac. It is surprising because they don't consciously set out to make a fortune. They aren't drawn to money, it is drawn to them. They won't sell their parents' house because it has so many sentimental memories associated with it. By the time they do come to sell, it is worth a small fortune. Cancer is also more likely to win money or be awarded money than other signs.

Cancerians can also work as mediators between separating couples who need a facilitator to work out the financial and practical end of the business. Many Cancerians are drawn to fabric, paint and interior decorations. They also make wonderful garden planners.

This basically shy sign can work brilliantly and very effectively with marginalised groups, especially in prison. This is where their caring, non-judgmental qualities are most evident.

That lady in the corner shop, or local supermarket, who always has a smile and bit of chat for you, and makes you feel like a special and individual person is probably a Cancerian!

GEMINI — This sign is the great talker of the zodiac. Talking is an art form; words are never bandied about with Geminians. They are well chosen and beautifully delivered, which is why so many Geminians make great actors. Gemini women are easy to spot at work; they move around a lot, chatting, catching up on gossip. They are attractively dressed; their hair is in the latest style and colour. They flirt, pick things up and put them down, drink coffee, offer biscuits and cheese around. The biscuits might be home made, the cheese might have been picked up at the French market they discovered in that little town in the country, that Gemini just happened to have hopped over to at the weekend. Does all this sound as though Gemini is at a party and not at work? Of course it does. That's what Gemini does best — party.

Gemini brigs a real joyous love of life to every situation. It's infectious. Ideas are exchanged with the morning greeting. A discussion about the time can turn into a discussion about whether or not foreign nationals should be allowed to vote. Within minutes everyone within earshot is involved in a discussion about civil liberties and human rights. The discussion could get quite heated with Gemini lady insisting that some political action should be taken, and what about organising a demonstration? And all this before the working day has even begun! Exhausting. Driven. Energetic. Ideas flowing. Words spilling out. Challenging. That's Gemini woman.

There are so many Gemini women in journalism, radio, television and magazines, that it is difficult to imagine how the whole media circus could survive without the massive Gemini input that is essential to its survival.

With the Gemini teacher in charge, every single student would have well and truly woken up within the first five minutes, feel alive, charged up and challenged to think. Gemini woman is marvellous at inspiring others to think, find out about the world they live in and do something about it. She is full of ideas about everything and can bring a different slant to just about every topic. It was probably a Gemini woman who first challenged the idea that a family was not just two parents — a mother and a father and their children — that a family was also the single mother and her child. It was probably a Gemini woman who insisted that a gay couple should have the same rights as any heterosexual couple. It isn't that she actually joined the political party and campaigned for a change in the law. She isn't an activist, but she got the idea circulated at grass roots level by insisting that the topic be discussed among family and friends, so that others were forced to think and maybe act on issues she raised.

The parent of a Gemini often despairs in the teenage years that the bright, articulate child seems to drift from job to job or course to course, starting something then dropping it quickly and moving on to something else. Gemini gets bored very easily and is difficult to motivate into staying long enough in a course or job to get a qualification or learn a particular task. This restless boredom is the essence of the Gemini personality. It does mean that eventually, Gemini has picked up many diverse skills in the first ten years of their working life and has acquired a very rounded education in the true sense of the word. Gemini would probably say, and feel, that they have a degree from the university of life itself.

Geminians are attracted to the theatre, film and television; to act, write, present, clean the place, work in the office or deliver the mail. They are expressive and artistic and enjoy being with a large number of people.

Geminians also like to travel. New languages are a stimulating challenge. But Gemini won't stop at picking up a few phrases. They want to find out how people in other countries live, where and how they shop, what they cook and eat. A job has to feel like a hobby, something they would do just for the fun of it. Money is not enough to tempt a Gemini woman into doing a job; she has to feel that it is fun, challenging and worthwhile. There is a very serious vein in her, running beneath that funny and fun-loving surface. She needs to feel that her work somehow benefits other people and makes some contribution to the human race. If she is off on holiday she may get wound up about the plight of women in another culture. She won't be a political activist in another country — she is too realistic and innately polite to openly interfere — but she'll write an article about it when she gets home, or a letter to the newspaper, or she'll phone a radio talk show. She won't do more than that, but she'll have motivated someone else to take action. By the time the action is being taken, Gemini woman has moved on to something else.

Gemini woman doesn't look for promotion, which surprises co-workers and the boss because the talents and abilities of a Gemini worker are evident very quickly. It's just that Gemini doesn't like too much responsibility. It ties her down. She needs to feel that she can move on at a moment's notice.

Gemini woman likes tackling anything where she has to use her mind. The software business is attractive because it offers the chance to solve problems and develop ideas. Geminians like working with money, or in buying and selling in some shape or form. The Gemini woman is ideally suited to sales. She looks good, instantly turns a sales situation into a social occasion, and seems to have a lot of fun as she is working. Her targets find her irresistible, and for the fifteen minutes she has spent with them, they feel alive and important.

Gemini woman should avoid physical work. It is draining and unrewarding and usually done very grudgingly. Gemini woman will either get someone else to do her housework or blitz it once a week. She doesn't mind living in a muddle; a chaotic kitchen seems a lot more fun to her than a neat and orderly one. She would far rather bring in her work and work mates to the kitchen, make gallons of coffee, treat them to her exotic food and plan the next work adventure.

Intuitive and psychic skills abound in this sign, and many really gifted astrologers, mediums and clairvoyants are Gemini. Gemini seems born with great insights into human nature and the human condition. As an astrologer or psychic, Gemini woman can see all the wonderful possibilities in another person and inspire them to go out and conquer their own world.

Gemini woman feels great depths of emotion and is capable of understanding other people's pain as well as joy. She could work very well and very understandingly as a marriage or relationship counsellor. She also makes a great Agony Aunt for a paper or magazine because apart from understanding the nature of the emotional problems she is dealing with, she is prepared to look for unconventional solutions to fit a particular problem.

Gemini woman brings her brand of charm, humour and understanding to each and every situation she is in. Looking down from high above and watching Gemini woman, anyone would have to understand and see that she is always working. I'm not talking about her nine to five paid work. I'm talking about all her activities from the moment she wakes in the morning until the moment she puts her head on the pillow at night. She talks, inspires, motivates, listens to other people. She has spent her day being an unpaid but very effective counsellor, therapist, guide, advisor and friend.

Completely different to Gemini is the sign of CAPRICORN. It is difficult to think of Capricorn in any setting other than the work setting. Work and Capricorn go together. Capricorn was born with the work ethic firmly in place. Capricorns are born ambitious and show an appetite for work even as a small child. Capricorns like physical work, brain work, any sort of work. Capricorn women make great managers. They actually enjoy responsibility and take it on quite early in their careers. They can turn their capable hands to anything, and can bring order to chaos. Capricorn woman has a practical mind and gets her priorities in good order. She has sound judgement too. Capricorn women get the best education they can and then set about using it to their best advantage. When she learns to drive, she won't rely on a friend or relative to teach her. Even if she has very little money, she will find the best professional driving instructor and learn from him or her.

If she is going to work in a shop, she will have studied that shop and walked around it several times before she has put in her application for an interview. She prepares herself for her working life with meticulous care. If she is going for an interview, she will find out where the interview is taking place in advance. She will find out how to get there a week in advance. Nothing is left to chance. She will also have found out as much as she possibly can about the workplace. She will arrive early for her interview and will have done all her homework, looking up the potential employer on the internet and finding out as much as she can about the history of the organisation, its present status and aims. She will dress in a well-groomed, low-key style, and not a single hair will be out of place. Her dress sense will be formal but feminine, her make-up spare, and if she wears any accessory, it will be expensive but minimal. She presents herself as a working woman, ready to start at a moment's notice.

There is nothing deceptive abut this appearance because Capricorn woman is the workaholic of the zodiac. She loves work. Whether she is working as a cook, an administrator, a delivery woman or a stockbroker, and she is capable of doing all these jobs, the more work she is given the better. Capricorn women like working in large organisations because it gives them a chance to climb steadily up the ladder to the top. The Capricorn woman who starts her working life filling the shelves in the supermarket has the private aim of managing the place as soon as she is given the opportunity. She will use her eyes and ears to find out who is the most important person in the place and work to please that person. She understands why there are rules and regulations. She respects the rules of the organisation and understands instinctively that no rules mean no effective organisation. She won't waste her time bucking the system or trying to change things. She works quietly and co-operatively to make the system work for her.

You won't find the Capricorn woman hanging around the coffee machine first thing in the morning, having a gossip about what went on the night before, or wondering who is going out with whom. She gets straight down to her work. She has probably done more in her first hour than other employees will get through in the whole day. It is absolutely no wonder that she impresses the boss so easily.

Working with systems rather than people has appeal for her. She is seen at her best in management. Running a golf club draws on all her skills. She can manage the members, knows how to price membership fees, can find staff to run the kitchen and draw up the budget efficiently, knows how to supervise outdoor staff, and can cope with every tiny detail with deadly efficiency. It will be profitable; she will make sure of that. She won't make changes. She won't alarm the predominantly male members with bouts of feminism. It is her special tribute that she can move about in and manage beautifully this predominantly male institution without anyone being aware that she is anything but the best manager the place has ever had.

Capricorn woman likes making money. She has a healthy respect for it. If some enterprise is not making money and showing a rising profit, she will act to make change. Capricorn also likes a well-defined career path and will work hard to achieve it.

This sign is connected to bones and teeth, so it is not surprising that a lot of Capricorns head into dentistry, either as a dentist, a dental hygienist, nurse or receptionist. Capricorn likes tradition and the traditional occupation of law and banking. Any institution to do with finance is attractive to Capricorn women.

Capricorn is also heavily associated with building and construction, and Capricorn women do very well at all organisational levels of construction and valuation. Not that selling is a strong point with Capricorn women. They don't seem to like actual selling. Maybe it is to do with the fact that they aren't really people-persons, or maybe there is some innate dislike of the sort of the actual face-to-face business of asking another person for money. Capricorn is better at keeping the books, fixing the price, working in the background.

If you want something done, like getting a house built, that means searching for the site, getting the planning permission, keeping within budget, seeing through to the finish a beautiful solid, long lasting product, then turn the whole business over to a Capricorn woman.

The insurance business also appeals to Capricorn women. Insurance makes solid sense. It is right that people should look to the future and make provision for themselves and their dependants. It is only fair that each individual should take care of themselves and not expect anyone else to shoulder their responsibilities. They understand what insurance is all about and approve the aims and work of the organisation.

Where Capricorn has to come into contact with people in the workplace, she is always at her happiest if the other people are also hard-working and ambitious. She detests idleness or sloppiness, because apart from time wasting, it isn't necessary. She won't tolerate it and this innately shy woman will assert herself to point out her views on these workplace faults. It won't make her popular, but that won't worry her. She doesn't go to work to win popularity polls. She goes to work to deliver a fair contribution for a fair wage.

As an employee she is just, fair, industrious, and expects to be well-rewarded in return.

Another sign that has Capricorn's ability to get to the top of the organisation is SCORPIO. But Scorpio has a different tour to the top and different motivation than Capricorn.

SCORPIO women are challenging, competitive and very tough. Scorpio likes power. Scorpio enjoys being in control. All of these qualities are well-hidden beneath a very sweet face dominated by intense and magnetic eyes. Most people are so captivated by the appearance and charisma of the Scorpio woman that they find themselves telling her their innermost secrets. Secrecy and hidden matters dominate Scorpio lives and Scorpios are often attracted to work of a secret, hidden, or highly confidential nature.

Police work attracts them, or work with the armed services, especially that of a hidden nature. Some of the best spies are said to emerge from the sign of Scorpio. Maybe Scorpio and Aquarius should combine in running that detective agency, especially when it organises high level security.

There are so many diverse and hidden qualities in Scorpio that no one job could encompass them easily. One of the reasons that Scorpio is drawn to police work is that this woman likes uncovering mysteries and digging out secrets. She is also very loyal and protective, so there are many aspects of police or security work that attract her.

But she is also drawn to power. In her own right she is a powerful personality who enjoys control — I won't say controlling people, because that makes her sound manipulative — over peoples' lives. She can be a force for good, if the circumstances are right.

Scorpio is also the sign of getting rid of unwanted things, so she works happily in a charity shop, or a waste disposal place. She has no fear of anything and everything fascinates her. She seeks knowledge. She loves coming across a new word. She rolls it around her tongue, speaking it, whispering it, singing it, finding out how many other people share her new knowledge. With her love of words and charismatic personality, she makes an awe-inspiring actress. Her electrifying personality comes through the lens and she photographs and films well. On the other side of the camera she manages to capture the essence of any person she is filming or photographing. Scorpio lady doesn't have to wriggle either truth or essence from anyone, it is something people find themselves willing to hand over.

Scorpio is also the sign of death and regeneration, so it's no surprise to find Scorpios working at forensic medicine or birth in some capacity or other. The fascination that death and the hereafter hold for Scorpio is almost a chapter in itself. Scorpios wonder about death, how people die, why they die, what happens afterwards. They are aware of the soul and often speculate about its journey through time. Working as a medium comes very naturally to some Scorpios. Other Scorpios dismiss the idea of life after death. But you can be sure that all Scorpios have thought about it and have a theory about it.

Scorpio keeps her secrets well hidden. You would have to know her a very long time before she opens up and talks about her inner being and deepest thoughts. She thinks deeply about people, their motives, their secret desires and the things they suppress or fantasise about. But she is also a deeply caring person and has a sincere wish to make people happy. For that reason she makes an excellent therapist. She reads people quickly and intuitively. It is impossible to lie to a Scorpio. They feel an untruth. Scorpio may not actually say anything, but there is something in that steady mesmeric gaze that lets the other know that she is well aware of the lie. Scorpio's skill and success as a counsellor, therapist or psychiatrist is the uncanny knack of getting the other person to be truthful to the self, allowing them to glimpse into their own flawed nature and be comfortable about it. Scorpio is fascinated, as I have said, by other people. Scorpio also has the belief that almost every human being is good and has something unique and good to offer to the world. The therapeutic success is in managing to convince the other person of just that.

Scorpio is attracted to money and power, and armed with both, puts them to very good use. Scorpio can be that fairy godmother in your life because she can be fantastically generous. If you need food, clothes, a lift to the airport, she'll meet that need. She is a very practical person and meets the practical and bodily needs first. If you need, but maybe don't realise it at the time, someone to listen to you, she's there. She gives that most valuable commodity; her time. She won't interrupt or criticise you, but gives you the space to find your own solutions. She is the ideal counsellor. You always leave her feeling much better about yourself.

Like Scorpio, **LEO** has an awareness of other peoples' problems. Leo, like Scorpio, is ambitious and likes to be in command. But Leo motivation is different. Leo woman feels she was born at the top, but by some accident of fate has found herself a little way down the pecking order. Leo likes people and can be very generous to friends. Leo is also very generous to herself. Admit it, Leo, you just love treating yourself to all the good things money can buy. If you think of the noble governor of a far flung province, or the Empress of a great dominion, you have the Leo personality. It radiates regularity. That is probably why so many Leo women get promoted to management posts at a relatively young age. They have the confidence and ability to manage and demonstrate this at an early opportunity in the workplace. Say, for instance a crisis arises at work. Leo knows how to deal with it. An example would be a situation where the boss didn't turn in. Leo wouldn't sit around waiting for instructions or waiting for something to happen. She would organise the work amongst other employees, deal with relaying information where necessary and find out as quickly as possible what had happened to the boss. The show would go on. Leo likes responsibility and takes it on quite naturally.

Leo sells very well. Put Leo into a very smart car salesroom and watch her compete with the men for title of Super Salesperson of the Year. Leo also enjoys selling fine art, antiques or expensive jewellery. Leo panders to no-one. That isn't an approach that appeals to them. They take command of the situation, and that includes the purchaser, and direct attention to the fine points of the item for sale with so much affection and reverence that the item becomes irresistible to the purchaser.

I have already said that Leo is an excellent manager and outstanding administrator, but what makes Leo so good at that sort of job is their ability to master a whole range of facts, needs and tasks. Leo also understands people. I have seen Leo bosses directing staff around as though they were performers in the circus and Leo the ringmaster. Yet no one seems to mind. They all run around slavishly obeying Leo, very anxious to earn that Big Cat's approval. The Lion is the animal associated with Leo, and Leo has all the arrogance and beauty of that animal.

Leo also has more than a fair share of artistic and creative abilities. They can draw, paint and photograph to a professional standard. They are very happy with artistic creation and very happy in the company of other creative people. They enjoy laughing and joking a lot, so any work that might deprive them of contact with people would be a mistake.

There are a sizeable number of Leos drawn to information technology, financial services and science. Scientific research doesn't particularly appeal but science applied to workplace technology, especially medical scientific technology, does appeal.

Leo girls need to cultivate patience in career matters. I have known really talented Leo girls who, if success doesn't happen instantly in their career, get disheartened, even depressed, and give up. If a young Leo girl feels like that, she should seriously consider starting up her own business. Starting a job agency, even a specialist one, might be a very good career option.

Leo has conviction and courage, as well as excellent sales skills and great personal magnetism. There is only one way Leo can go — straight to the top.

LIBRA isn't known as the workaholic of the zodiac. Many people think of Libra as being lazy because they appear to enjoy life so much. But Libra is very far from lazy. Libra is wise enough to seek out work they enjoy doing, and doing it with people they like being with. Libra is drawn to occupations where no confrontation is necessary. They like jobs or services that improve others' sense of well-being. The fact that they don't make a laboured song and dance about everything conceals the fact that they put in long hours at work, are always ready and willing to stay on at work to complete the task in hand, and don't bargain for extra pay for doing what they consider to be their work duty. Libra is generous in all things, with their time and their money.

Underlying this easy-going attitude to life, Libra has a very strong belief in justice, law and order, and is drawn to careers in the law, or some aspect of the legal system.

Librans are amongst the most physically beautiful and graceful of the zodiac. They love to watch a world become more beautiful under their artistic and kindly hands. They have an instinctively good taste in colour and decorate their homes artistically. They make wonderful interior designers, painters and decorators. As artists, they create wonderful paintings. They like people to look good and can always see room for improvement. Their skill in achieving this lies in the tactful personality always present in the non-confrontational nature of the Libran. The Libran woman hairdresser or beautician somehow brings about the magical make-over of her client whilst allowing the client to believe that she thought of it all herself. The Libran dressmaker creates the most desirable look for her client without ever pointing out that she has somehow managed to highlight the client's good points and conceal the not so good points. Modelling clothes is second nature to the Libran lady; she does it magnificently.

If Libran lady is cleaning her house or your house she manages to change some bits of furniture around without causing the least offence and creating the most beautiful and harmonious effect.

In other sorts of work using people skills rather than artistic skills, the Libran is extraordinarily effective. She manages to place the right person in the right job, can resolve conflict in organisations, and makes an excellent marriage counsellor. Libra has the knack of bringing about change in the way people think about themselves. Because she sees the good points and strong qualities she gets people to see this themselves and shows them the desirability of change.

A couple in need of relationship counselling find in the Libran counsellor an understanding ally. And a situation that started out as warlike is quickly diffused with the couple deciding that separation is desirable. The couple may leave the session the best of amicable friends, with the spoils of the relationship peacefully divided up.

These mediation skills, abundant in the Libran personality, are offered so tactfully that clients don't feel threatened or judged.

Libra is essentially working in the service of others. Libra doesn't want control over others, only a development and revelation of all that is good and best in each person. A patient nursed by a Libran feels that they are in the kind and loving hands of their own mother.

But the Libran has the organisational ability of a very good administrator too, even if they don't make a parade of it. The organisation is done coolly and logically, and above all else quietly, in their own head. What others see and receive is the action taking place after Libra has made a balanced judgement about what action is necessary. If Libra is the boss of a disruptive employee there won't be a scene or a public reprimand of the culprit. Libra will think about where that employee's talents could be better used. The potentially difficult situation will be quietly diffused.

If the Libran were running a hotel and in charge of someone in the office who never stopped talking, therefore preventing everyone else from getting on with other work, she would move the chatter-box to reception where her talking skills could be really useful. That's Libra in action.

The Libran lawyer won't act quickly or jump into unnecessary litigation. She will think it through, attempt to see the situation from every angle, and then come up with the most peaceful and usually effective judgement.

The Libran police officer will diffuse a violent situation by use of tact, charm and good humour.

Librans need to be appreciated in the workplace. Part of their satisfaction from the work is the feeling that their efforts are noticed and appreciated. They love their work and want to be loved in the workplace. A boss who takes them for granted or who thinks of them only as a number will hurt them deeply. Libra personalises the workplace, liking to bring in plants, flowers, photos, or cakes from home. Cooking is a great Libran skill. Food is cooked in an old-fashioned, homely way, but presented to the table with all the finest skill and artistry that can be mustered. It is then eaten in good company.

Librans have a real skill in running their own business. They have a feel for how and when to present their product. They attract people to them because they so obviously enjoy what they do. They enjoy making money, and money is attracted to this attractive sign. They enjoy hunting for bargains and getting the best possible value for money. Librans make excellent agents for others buying fine art, housekeeping, stocks and shares, clothes or furniture. Hire a Libran to furnish your house and garden and they'll do it with real enthusiasm in the best possible taste and at the best possible rate.

✿ **VIRGO** is a hardworking and almost completely honest sign. Virgo is also extremely efficient and if given free rein and trust by the boss, will always find a more efficient way of doing something.

Virgo can be an exacting task master, but they make very good teachers. Nothing on the syllabus will be omitted and the Virgoan teacher won't move onto the next item on the teaching agenda until they have satisfied their own very high standards and expectations. There aren't any frilly bits to the Virgo teacher, and they will not tolerate poor discipline or mockery. But their very earnest commitment to the business of teaching, and teaching well, impresses even the most difficult student and gains the necessary co-operation.

Virgo will slog it out in the office. They find information technology and all forms of computer work appealing. They like numbers and are very at home in the ordered world of accountancy and bookkeeping. They want to impress the boss and be noted for their devotion to duty and a willingness to complete the task in hand, no matter how many hours it takes. This sometimes makes them a target for the workplace bully. Some Virgoans suffer bullying in the workplace until their innate good manners give way to outrage and anger. This quietly spoken sign can then erupt into an angry spate of words that leaves the bully with no illusions. Before such fury, even the toughest of those addicted to bullying back down.

Virgoans take themselves very seriously, and as they get older, learn the wisdom of relaxing a bit more in the workplace. The quality of work doesn't suffer, but the more relaxed attitude means that Virgo enjoys it a bit more.

Virgoans work very well with their hands. They enjoy putting things together and respond well to the movement and discipline of factory work. As line-assembly factory supervisors they are excellent, because they have a great eye for small detail.

This eye for meticulous detail makes Virgo a very good bank employee. They can spot mistakes in procedures and figure work at first glance. They play things by the book because they believe the rule book was written for a good reason.

Virgoans also like to work in electronics. It satisfies them. They relate well to mechanised and electronic systems. An area in which all the Virgoan talents for method, order and implementation of the highest standards shine at their brightest is in health care.

Virgo is committed to good health for the self and for all. Every aspect of health — whether it's nursing, working in an office for a health department, health inspection, safety and cleanliness inspection, or any similar job — is attractive to Virgoans. More than any other sign, they understand that for the individual and the nation, good mental and physical health is wealth.

Virgoans can see where improvements must be made in private and public hygiene and will campaign tirelessly to bring improvement about. They make very able food and hygiene inspectors, and if given powers to prosecute wrongdoers will pursue them tirelessly.

They look at safety aspects of the workplace and point out areas of defect. The employee most likely to have a first aid qualification in the workplace is Virgo.

Virgo is drawn to work where the law backs and upholds what they are doing. Work as a traffic warden, litter person, or a policewoman attracts them. Virgo is attracted to uniformed work and works well in security, often in large department stores.

Working in large organisations is a safe and secure place for the Virgoan, who likes the reliability of the conditions and pay. But their wrath will be visited on anyone who is sloppy in their standard or approach, and they sometimes make themselves unpopular with other employees by pointing out co-workers' defects.

Because it is linked to good health, Virgo is often attracted to pest-control work, or work in sanitation and cleansing. Virgoans don't particularly like sales work but will work in that area if the sale involves any health or medical product. Insurance makes good sense to them, and they work in that area in any capacity, content in the knowledge that they are making a contribution to individual and national well-being.

Virgo believes that debts must be paid and those who run up debts are wrong, so they don't object to working as a debt collector.

Most Virgoans aren't keen on running their own business. They hate the unpredictably of it, not knowing if money will come in, or how much has to go out. They are shy about promoting themselves. They feel happier in a highly structured work environment where the job brief is spelled out.

Although Virgo is not innately artistic or creative, they can do well in health promotion. If asked to devise a campaign warning drinking drivers of the insanity of their action, Virgo can mount and target a very effective campaign. Virgo can also pester the right people persistently enough to get the money to run a sustained campaign.

The attention to detail and precision of the work makes collecting data for a census, or any official statistics collection, appealing.

Virgo is happiest at work when they know what they are doing and why it has to be done. One of the most valuable assets any employer could have is a Virgo employee.

Money

People have all sorts of different ideas about money. Some people are attracted to money, others are envious of it, to some it definitely does not make them happy, but it can be agreed that everyone needs it.

Lurching from one financial disaster to another is a miserable business. But so is a life of working hard and still never having enough to buy the basic necessities.

Some star signs plot early in life that they are going to devote themselves to making money. Others hoard up money, convinced that this makes them secure. Others hold onto money, finding the business of parting with it an unbearable wrench. Sagittarius likes gambling with money. Libra loves spending money. Scorpio is attracted to monied people, seeing them as powerful beings. Cancerians like money to buy the biggest and squashiest sofa in the shop as a comforting nest in the home. Pisces throws money away and feels that they have been unlucky, not unwise. Capricorn can be so stingy with money it's remarkable that they display anything elegant on their person or home.

Each sign has its strengths and weaknesses with money. A few signs are genuinely lucky and money seems to follow them around. Other signs can make money work very well for them.

Through my radio show, and in dealings on a face to face basis with clients, I have come to understand each sign and the way those signs relate to money. Here are some of the insights I have gained over the years.

≋ **PISCES** has a completely different approach to money than Leo. Pisceans seem to muddle through financially. They have all the artistic talent to make plenty of money, but not the drive or confidence. Pisces is quite content to go from pay day to pay day, rarely thinking too far ahead. Young Pisceans would think that getting a trip to the moon would be more realistic than taking out a pension. Pisceans live very much in the here and now. They spend money on the next enjoyable moment; in the pub, in the boutique, on that delicious meal or that holiday in the sun. The pleasure is the reward. As the money runs down, trickling into a few cent between then and the next pay day, they manage to cope. They may make a half-hearted promise that it will be different next week, or maybe next month, but it rarely is. Pisces simply love shopping and, for them, it really is therapy. They know that there will be an anxiety about running out later, but later is a long way off. Pisces is also very generous. Christmas shopping for relatives and friends is a real pleasure. Pisces only wishes she had a lot more money to splash out on all the people she loves. And Pisces loves a lot of people.

Pisces is very uneasy about borrowing. They just don't like it, and the weight of debt is heavy on them. With very great reluctance will they accept a loan from a friend and they always repay it as quickly as possible.

There is a sense of honour in the Piscean make-up about money. If they don't have it, they don't borrow it. The only exception to this self-imposed rule is the Piscean who is addicted to drink, drugs or alcohol. Then the addiction suppresses the normal Piscean instincts.

Pisces manages to stretch a small budget in many directions, especially when they have young children. The food is always varied and healthy, the clothes are good and stylish, the house is warm. Everyone at home is happy.

Pisces isn't a financial magician though. Far from it. But Pisces can be happy with very little. And because Pisces radiates happiness and contentment with little, the rest of the household is happy too. Pisces won't complain that she hasn't got a car. She will cheerfully get herself onto a bike, or if she has children, load them all onto the nearest bus. Pisces will carry all her shopping from the supermarket home without any idea that she is to be pitied. When she does get her first car she is as thrilled as a child with a new and exciting toy for Christmas.

She is never envious of others with more money; she simply wishes them well.

Yet money follows Pisces around. There is always someone willing to give them a job. They can be lucky in getting property, but they are just grateful to have a sound roof overhead. If luck does exist, then it visits Pisces at least once or twice in the lifetime. Pisces is one of the signs most likely to have a big win on either the National Lottery, an inspired gamble, or from a Prize

Bond. A friend, spouse or family member may offer to share a win with them.

Pisces is also likely to be given a business to run. It may be handed over by a family member, or Pisces may just happen to be in the right place at the right time and pick up a business easily or cheaply.

I've often felt that because Pisces is such a generous and giving sign that the universe pays them back. When circumstances are sound and secure and the Piscean feels confident, they really do glow with contentment and never take it for granted. Because they feel lucky about money, they often are. Yet in reality, their demands of financial life are very few. Money isn't what makes the Piscean happy. People do that. Life does that.

ARIES woman has a very complex relationship with money. When she is battling away with a mountain of domestic bills, with maybe rent or a mortgage to pay and either not enough or barely enough to manage on, one part of her is oppressed by the constant nagging anxiety about money. The other part of her is challenged and pleased at her ability to cope. By nature she is thrifty; some might say stingy. To her, it doesn't make sense to book a holiday and pay for it by credit card. Aries is one of the least likely of the zodiac signs to run up credit card debt. If debts do loom close, she takes instant action, reducing expenditure to avert the crisis. She is quite able to do without. It is in her nature to make do with what she has. If she was partnered with someone who spends freely or allows debt to mount up, it would lead to very serious rows and probably the breakdown of the relationship. Her money will go into property. She will furnish it as and when she has the money. She will go for years with the same kitchen or bathroom as long as it remains functional. Anyone tearing out a perfectly good working kitchen and spending a lot of money on modernisation, or a more fashionable effect at great expense, is absolutely insane in her eyes. If that feckless spender moans about not having money afterwards, she gets no sympathy whatsoever from Miss Aries.

She will only spend if she has to. As soon as possible, she begins a small savings scheme and regularly tucks money away. She expects functional value from clothes and enjoys the challenge of buying what she needs as cheaply as she can. Her car is merely the means of getting her from one place to another. Unless it was a necessity, she would not dream of looking for extravagant car finance. She would not be impressed with herself if she did that, and couldn't care less about creating an impression to suit other people. She is her own person and that is all that counts.

She doesn't expect to have more out of her financial life than she is capable of earning. There are no daydreams about a large win, or some mystery inheritance, or somehow having a financial windfall. She is entirely practical and realistic in recognising that you only have what you earn, and that spending more each month than what comes in leads to serious life difficulties.

Even when she is better off financially and has money saved, she keeps her habits of thrift. She is not a likely lotto winner, money is not attracted to her, but if she did win, it would not change her at all. She is and will always be entirely grounded.

Like Aries, ✺ **SAGITTARIUS** is a fire sign, but has a very different approach to money. It is a pity that Sagittarius couldn't take at least one leaf from the Aries book of expenditure. Most Sagittarians feel lucky a lot of the time, and in fact are luckier than most others in the zodiac. Money is attracted to Sagittarius; money making opportunities present themselves early in life. Many Sagittarians have a second string to their financial bow in the form of a hobby that pays, or a second job. Windfalls seem to arrive at fairly regular intervals but as soon as Sagittarius knows the windfall is on the way, the money is spent in the mind, as Sagittarius suddenly discovers a pressing financial need (like a holiday in the sun) that they didn't know existed the day before. Sagittarius is an impulse buyer. Those beautiful floor tiles spotted in the shop as she is dashing to the dentist suddenly become something her home can't do without. The already perfectly good floor must instantly be taken up and the lovely new tiles put down. She is happy, ecstatic. That gorgeous but outrageously expensive outfit in the window obsesses her until it is bought, with cash, a credit card, money borrowed from her mother, whatever, who cares? Feelings of longing can't be assuaged until the outfit is hers.

A few bills come in and are put to one side to be dealt with later as the rent or mortgage must be paid. Feeling a bit down, she throws a party or has a few friends over for a wonderful supper where the atmosphere is friendly and convivial, the food great and the wine flowing freely. That's what life is about, she tells herself, living in and for the moment. Her friend is having financial difficulties, so generous to a fault, Sagittarius woman digs into her purse and doles out a loan, gift, whatever. 'Pay me back when you can.' She can't bear to see someone she cares about stressed out over something as trivial as money. Her child or partner has a longing for that special Christmas or birthday present, but why wait for Christmas or a birthday? She rushes out to get it now.

The bills pour in, the letters marked FINAL REMINDER arrive. A few economies are practised for a day or so. The seriousness of the situation doesn't strike her. It is other people reminding her she owes money, or demanding money which must be paid immediately that prompts her into action. Cleverly and briskly she copes with the problems by negotiating a loan to pay all her debts and give her a little money to spend. She spends it probably the day after the loan money is lodged to her account. Then she forgets that the repayment debt will be taken out of her bank account every single month. If she didn't have enough money each week or each month to pay all her bills, she has even less now. The logic doesn't penetrate that optimistic Sagittarian head. Then what she has been expecting all along happens; that windfall arrives.

Money is attracted to Miss Sagittarius. If financial sense were as attracted, she might be a very wealthy woman. The financial universe treats her very kindly. She gambles and wins and quickly forgets the nightmare of the poverty and financial ruin that so often threatened her.

Many Sagittarians, through luck and definitely not providence, somehow end up well-to-do and spending recklessly all their lives. That part of that recklessness is a generosity and the willingness to work hard at just about anything is the redeeming grace of this sign.

🐟 AQUARIUS shares some of these Sagittarian traits. She would like to be a lavish spender because it feels good to have all the goodies of life, but Aquarius doesn't put much store on having things to display to impress other people. Aquarius likes to impress Aquarius. She enjoys experimenting with life. The idea of running her own business attracts her because of the challenge it makes to her ingenuity. If she makes money, and she is capable of making a great deal of money, it is a bonus. She is drawn to risk taking, even a business gamble, but she is averse to taking the advice of an older and wiser head, because she likes to do things her way. If it doesn't work out, she shrugs and moves on to the next venture. She learns from her own mistakes. She is often drawn to large money-making enterprises where her verbal talents get her into a position where her ideas are listened to and she finds herself with a well-paid position of responsibility. She enjoys the prestige and is casually appreciative of the money she makes but, on a whim, can walk away from it all because some other job or enterprise beckons.

She has charm, wit and style, and she likes doing things on a grand scale, often attracting a wealthy partner, or a man who plans to be wealthy. She enters into all his business schemes and plans with interest and energy. She helps him make money. It excites her. She sometimes puts money by, but will withdraw and spend it on some piece of latest technology — a fantastic music system, a new computer, the latest technological toy — whatever takes her whimsical fancy.

She is very good at standing back and seeing where and how money can be made, and she invests time and energy into working out her money-making plan. It is the planning, talking and watching her ideas in action that excites her. If she makes enough money, she might go for a second property as an investment because it seems like a good idea on a particular day, and not with any idea of being wealthy and secure in the future.

Yet somehow financial life is kind to Aquarians and they usually end up with all the home and financial security they need without ever having made any plans for it. They take money for granted. If there is no money, they will put their very able wits towards making what is needed.

🐏 **CAPRICORN** couldn't be more different in approach. The Aquarian approach is far too erratic for Capricorn. All Capricorns like good quality things in home furnishings, clothes, cars and property. The way to have all those nice things is to have the money with which to pay. Money comes from work; sensible, solid and reliable work. There are no great universal plans for provision of money or possessions; the planning is done in the head of the individual. Capricorn is logical and realistic. A well-paid job leads quickly to an affordable mortgage. The investment in home furnishings is going to be made once and will be on things that last. Money will be budgeted for the best quality possessions. The word and concept, 'possession' is crucial to understanding the Capricorn relationship to money. *It is mine, I own it, it belongs to me, no one is taking it away from me. I will fight vigorously to defend the things I own, the things I have worked for.* The making of money, and the spending of it, is closely tied in to the Capricorn woman's view of herself. It is to do with self-respect. She is, in essence, a respectable woman and she respects herself. In making money, spending it wisely and putting money away for her future, she is showing herself respect.

If somehow she only has low-paid work, she will still work very hard to surround herself with good quality things. Her home will be solid, conventional and beautiful.

She looks always to securing her financial future, comfort and security. She does not expect anyone else to pay. She is self-reliant. She likes planning and knowing that her plan will succeed. She won't take any chances. She is an excellent employee and a very good business woman. If she starts her own business, because it will give her more money, there will be little element of gamble involved. If anyone is going to exploit the labour contribution she makes, she is going to be top of the list.

Taking out a pension early in adulthood makes sense to her. She understands that if she wants something, and she wants a lot out of life, it is up to her to provide it. She won't spend money on holiday apartments or hotels; she'll buy her own holiday apartment in whatever country or resort she goes to. She is a creature of habit, so she knows she will always go on liking the same holiday resort.

In the event of a relationship breakdown, she will contest with energy any attempt made by her partner to take away money, property or possessions. It is the only time when she may act uncharacteristically in other peoples' eyes. Others may wonder why she is prepared to spend so much on legal fees to battle it out with an ex partner. The fees are only going to be paid out of the joint assets, so why deplete them with unnecessary litigation? It is because Capricorn woman could not live with herself if she didn't make every attempt to hold on to everything. It damages her self-respect. But she will emerge from any legal or financial battle with her self-respect and financial security intact.

LEO woman is often quite like Capricorn woman in physical appearance and her liking for first class possessions. But her love of good quality and the finer things life has to offer is not outweighed by what she has to do to get them. Leos love the things that money can buy. They like the best quality food eaten in good restaurants. Even when financial times are quite hard for Leo, a meal eaten in a stylish restaurant in good company is money well spent. If Leo wants something for the home, she will wait until she can afford the best before investing. She will often put up with a shabby kitchen or bathroom for a long time before that investment is made. It is extremely unlikely that she will borrow for her dream. Leo borrowing is done on a strictly 'need' basis.

Leo woman has to like her work, even if it is not well-paid. She prefers to like it rather than be highly paid for it. If she starts her own business, it will be because she is prompted by a desire to be the manager or the owner, rather than because it will make her a lot of money. But she is attracted to wealth and is drawn to men who are powerful and well-off. A well-off, powerful man has all the mental and physical qualities to hold her attention. The money is a bonus. She is a very grounded person and dislikes getting into debt. It worries her and causes her sleepless nights. A few financial mistakes — living with a large credit card bill or enduring the shame of admitting to a creditor that she hasn't the money to pay her own bills — is a sufficiently humiliating experience to ensure that it does not happen again. Leo woman learns from her financial mistakes.

Leo woman was born to be the spouse of a man of wealth. She looks like a millionaire's wife, and has all the regal charm and sumptuous appearance of a woman of wealth and influence, even when she earns little money.

Good quality clothes of distinction have great appeal for Leos. The clothes don't have to carry a designer label, unless that designer genuinely produces clothes of superlative quality. And to lay hands on those clothes, Leo is just as happy to pick them up in a charity shop.

What Leo hates is the naked display of money and what it can buy. There is something innately distasteful to Leo's refinement in the vulgar display of wealth. Leo won't talk much about money. They will neither try to win your sympathy by moaning about being broke nor offend you by bragging about how much money they made last year. Only occasionally will Leo gamble. They might enjoy an outing to the races for the joy of being in the open air and watching thoroughbred horses run and compete. They may enjoy putting a few Euro on a horse, but would never lay on a large bet because someone has told them that the horse in question is a sure thing. Leo won't squander money. They want value for it.

Her secret driving force is that, deep down, she believes she was born to be rich. Her poverty is temporary, accidental. One day she will have all the money she needs. It does eventually come to her. Wealth and poverty are both relative concepts, so defining what wealth or poverty means is individual to Leo. One woman may end up with that cottage in the country she dreamed of as a little girl. Another will find herself going on that expensive but fabulous safari she took so often in her youthful imagination. Another may one day wear that amazing and very large diamond ring she always knew was her birthright. Another may win a large amount of money.

One way or another, Leo woman will have the things she secretly dreamed of. Her secret dreams were always a future glimpse of what the universe had in store for her.

Leo can be a generous supporter of charity causes but is unlikely to be hoodwinked into parting with cash for something they consider a scam, or just plain profiteering. Leo is far too canny to get involved in pyramid selling and has a fair idea of where the profits in that type of enterprise go. Unless Leo is born to wealthy parents, or inherits a business, large sums of money rarely come their way. If they really want a lot of money, Leo can and will set up a business, manage it well, and make the fortune that way.

If **TAURUS** could only share in the secret of Leonine belief in the ability of the universe to one day pay up, they wouldn't suffer so many doses of the 'poor me's'. Taurus is driven by a secret fear that all the good things they have and have worked so hard to secure will be swept away from them if they don't keep looking back over their shoulder. Taurus also suffers from the desire to have a bit more. Whatever they have is never quite enough. There is always something else out there. The house might be lovely, and Taurus has really good homemaking skills, but one morning Taurus will come down to breakfast and realise that the house is not quite big enough. The mission starts to find somewhere bigger.

If Taurus is single it's straightforward enough; she looks at the buying or renting options and makes arrangements. She doesn't need to persuade herself because she saw in a flash that the place that was perfectly satisfactory yesterday is no longer adequate. The trouble starts when she has to convince her partner that they need, if she is to be happy, a bigger place, with a classy neighbourhood thrown in for good measure. Unless he is a man of iron and can withstand the constant talk, he will have to give in for the sake of domestic peace.

A car that's just four wheels and an engine won't do. Why should it when that great shiny solid model is waiting for her in the showroom?

She will stretch her budget to meet all these financial needs, but moan ceaselessly when, as is inevitable, she is constantly broke. She feels pity for herself; she is a hard worker, always pays her way, and yet here she is, not able to afford a holiday. How is it that the woman she works with is able to go away twice a year to Turkey or Spain, and she can't get to take a weekend away in a hotel? How is it that she is at a financial stretch when she has practised the most stringent household economies? The woman next door wouldn't lower herself to do any such thing.

Taurean woman is appalled if her spouse or mother suggests that she sell her big apartment or house and move into something smaller and more affordable. She behaves as though she is about to be evicted in her bare feet. These well-meant suggestions only confirm her secret fear of eviction, of looming poverty, of social disgrace. In her innermost being she does not feel lucky, does not believe in a higher power that would be only too happy to send her all she needs if only she would trustingly ask.

She feels unlucky and deeply fears that unless she works very hard to avert financial disaster, life will try to make a fool of her.

Of course she holds on to her comfortable home and there is always good food on the table, and everyone in her home is taken very good care of, and she is extremely unlikely to suffer poverty in old age, but inside she never loses her fear of being in want, or her belief that she is poor.

♊ **VIRGO** shares some of these secret Taurean fears. But Virgo is a very practical sign with a very good relationship with money. Virgo wants security and that security lies in having her basic needs met. As long as she can live in a secure environment where she can live peacefully and have enough money to buy food to nourish her, and heating to keep her warm, she is content. Virgo is a hard worker and respects the money she earns. She will only buy what she can afford, and if taking out a mortgage will check, re-check and take advice on the mortgage that lies well within her financial budget and projected future earnings. She will also make sure that there is adequate insurance to pay for the mortgage in case anticipated disaster strikes, like losing a job or becoming ill. She looks ahead. That is her principal financial strength.

She anticipates the worst possible scenario and prepares for it. The financial future holds no terror for her. What creates a financial nightmare for her is having a partner or family member for whom she is responsible, with a problem or addiction that creates financial chaos. She is torn between the loyalty demanded by love and the constant headache of not knowing what financial madness the demon of addiction will create for tomorrow. Virgo is a loyal and faithful sign, but if a loved one continues to create financial chaos then love dies. The practical Virgoan brain assumes control of the situation and encourages some very tough love. The miscreant can shape up or ship out.

In the Virgoan mind, financial control means peace of mind and the calmness that living sanely brings. This very mild and essentially peace-loving sign can become as ferocious as the toughest warrior if the financial stability of life is under constant threat. The situation is ended. Peace reigns once again and Virgo is happy.

♊ **GEMINI** is a happy sign too, but for very different reasons. Virgoan happiness and sanity is a very different affair to what drives Gemini. Gemini does not want anything to interfere with the joy of living each day as it comes. Gemini wants to work in a social environment, and socialise with innumerable friends, acquaintances and family members when they are around. Money makes all that a much happier affair. The Gemini is usually a physically attractive person with a stunning personality, but not in the least bit conscious of how they look. They like to look in the current fashion but don't care about how much or how little it costs. The look is achieved accidentally, but they get there. The home can be large or small, rented or bought; it doesn't matter as long as it contains a bed to sleep in every night. It is only as they get older that they start looking for the security of a home they won't have to move from and can afford, often in their forties. Bills are paid as and when Gemini has the money. They think borrowing a very useful thing. It bails them out of financial difficulties.

They never actually feel that there is a financial crisis, so don't agonise over it. While they have energy, they can work for what they need. There is often a parent or two around who will loan them money, or a bank to be accommodating over any little temporary difficulty. If the home looks chaotic you can be sure the Gemini finances are in the same state. That film festival in Italy? Looks like a marvellous idea! And just look at that special online offer of a cheap flight and hostel accommodation! Book it now and let's go.

If there is a spouse around, Gemini shamelessly hands over the nightmare of bringing order into financial chaos and continues on. Gemini wants no interruption to the essential business of enjoying life. If confronted with financial reality she is repentant and makes umpteen promises to make amends. At the time she really means to adhere to all these promises.

At the back of her mind is the secure knowledge that at any moment she chooses she can stop, think, use her agile brain and hit on some scheme to make enough money to resolve all her financial difficulties. She keeps this secret weapon to herself. Because while she keeps up her apparent child-like ignorance about, and attitude towards money, she gets away with financial murder.

Her success lies in the fact that she rarely pushes things to the brink of financial disaster. She knows the financial and emotional limits of anyone she relies on to bail her out of her difficulties, and knows that she is well able to turn her finances around whenever the moment is right.

For a sign so addicted to enjoying the social life that money facilitates, she is rarely drawn to marrying or living with a wealthy man. One part of her despises people who are slaves to making money. She is cynical about the motivation and character make-up of people who use their money to dominate or impress. Anyone who displays wealth is vulgar.

Whilst she might feel that the universe owes her a living, she doesn't harbour any secret hope or wish that the universe is about to reward her with a windfall. Yet she is one of the signs of the zodiac quite likely to win or inherit money. It is as though the universe is saying to her that it approves of her wholehearted enjoyment of life. It likes the way she spends money, it approves of her spreading so much light-hearted fun amongst her friends and family and is giving her the wherewithal to carry on. When her big cheques arrive you can hear her laughing as she sits down to plan another big and very successful party.

CANCER woman would sooner die than squander her money on a big party when there are bills to be paid and the children's education to be planned. She is thrifty, sensible and the bank manager's dream. Yet in her own way, Cancerian woman is as complex in her attitudes to money as Aries woman. Security is what she is about. Every penny must be directed into the home. Everyone must earn their keep and make a contribution to the smooth and uncomplicated running of the home. Buying an expensive television and sound system makes sense because it is, at the end of the day, a cheap form of entertainment to be enjoyed by the family as a group. But the idea of having an expensive holiday and living on chips to pay for it afterwards offends her idea of herself as a nurturer and provider of home comfort. Comfort lies in being able to afford things. Going into debt creates serious worries for her and can make her physically ill. A bill she can't pay gives her, literally, a headache.

She is self-reliant; something overlooked in this essentially feminine sign. She is prepared to work very hard both in and outside the home to pay for home essentials and comforts. She has an excellent brain and shrewd business sense, and her investments are likely to be in education. That educational advantage will secure a good living, and provide financially for the future. She will run jewellery parties from home to make extra money, and Cancerian woman was probably the first to hold a Tupperware party.

She will spend on clothes, make-up and oceans of gorgeous perfume, but only when she has paid her bills and laid enough aside for the next round of bills.

She puts a little aside to anticipate Christmas, birthdays and that wedding coming up in August. She hoards up clothes, unused birthday cards, and leftover Christmas wrapping paper for use next time around. She takes such good care of things that they rarely need replacing, so she isn't out buying new furniture or carpets on a regular basis. Besides which, she is sentimentally attached to her possessions. She is the ideal financial wizard. Her money saving skills are evident in the home, and her considerable money making skills are evident outside the home. Her savings are there for that rainy day. She takes sound advice from those she trusts, and acts on it. If financial disaster strikes, in the form of a failed business, she doesn't sit around feeling sorry for herself. She goes to work for someone else. She has no pride in that respect, just sound common sense.

She is a financial winner. The universe frequently rewards her with a win or unexpected lump sum and windfalls regularly find their way to her door.

LIBRA is rarely poor, because Libra is a very hard-working sign. Libra loves spending money, but Librans also appreciate that money has to be earned. Librans are also great financial planners and can organise their own and anyone else's finances almost miraculously. But there is a curious aberration in the Libran make-up. Secretly, Libra lives in dread that their home, money and financial security will be swept away. Librans often go on working longer and harder than other signs because of this secret fear. The up-side of this is that Librans stack away enough financial security to guarantee a comfortable old age. But in reality, Libra has often made enough money to retire early.

Libra has the knack of spotting good value in property and often buys cheaply, and uses that fabulous sense of interior and exterior design to turn a cheap property into a valuable one. Libra often goes on to get a second property as an investment. Nothing too big, nothing too expensive, but something sensible and providing financial security for old age.

Libra is one of the best signs of the zodiac for spotting bargains and pouncing on them. I have seen numerous Libran friends just arrive at the door of a large department store – clothes department of course – and move as though miraculously to the one real bargain in the place. Libra loves designer labels, but gets a real thrill out of getting them at bargain basement rates.

Libran women are very generous to their families and friends, and can't bear to see them in need. They help out with loans, property and even hand over their savings to children about to start up a business. But Libra really needs to get it clear that the money is a loan and not a gift. If the money is not repaid, Libran woman is angry and resentful.

Her natural generosity and kindliness makes her offer loans and financial help, but her secret insecurities about money also cause her to feel fear and resentment about parting with cash. The best financial advice to give Libran women is to stop and think before making that offer.

Libran women aren't lucky when it comes to winning money but they are lucky in landing money-making opportunities. So, although Libran woman often worries about money, she is rarely in financial difficulties – her sense of balanced spending and planning is too good.

SCORPIO woman is much luckier than Libran woman. Scorpio women are attracted to money and to money-making men. A well-to-do man is like a magnet to Scorpio woman. She identifies being rich with being powerful. She loves that sense of freedom and choice that having money brings. It isn't that she will join her Libran sister on massive shopping trips; she won't. Scorpio woman can live very thriftily and simply. Her cooking is simple and healthy, her dress sense simple and sensual. Jewellery usually has a sentimental association. She won't look for diamonds and rubies unless they are symbols of love.

She is a worker, but she won't kill herself or be a workaholic. Yet money is attracted to her as she is attracted to it. Scorpio woman will marry money if she can. She will be attracted by a man with his own business. Money is power and power is a sexual turn-on. She flirts with money and often enjoys a gamble. That elegant woman in black, with a sweep of blonde hair and a single diamond at her throat, playing the roulette table in the casino, is likely to be a Scorpio woman at play.

Scorpio woman often wins money, and when she makes a money wish it is often granted. It's all to do with the way the Scorpio thinks about the universe. She has psychic and magnetic powers. She also believes that she was meant to be rich (in much the same way as Leo woman does) and that the universe had better start delivering the money she is calmly expecting. It is no surprise to hear that what she wants and has wished for arrives. It staggers other people to hear her casually mentioning that she wants a big house with a very private garden and a holiday home in Tenerife, and ten years later she has all she wished for.

Scorpio woman can be secretive and even selfish about money. She won't admit she has it, and won't part with it unless it's for her spouse or children. They have first call (about ten lengths after herself) and she rarely grudges parting with money where love is concerned.

She has the ability, when she has to, of living without money, or very little anyway. If she has to budget tightly during a time of financial hardship, you'll rarely hear her moaning or indulging in the poor-little-me's. She gets on with it. She's even stylish about her poverty.

There is always a touch of magic about Scorpio woman, and when she waves her sparkly wand and makes a wish for money, it happens.

HEALTH

Health

In this section I want to show the link between the sign of the zodiac and the health of the individual. Each of the twelve signs governs a different part of the body. The sign of Taurus, for example, governs the throat. I know that all signs get sore throats from time to time, but I have learned in the course of my psychic career that Taureans suffer more than most. Also, I have come to recognise, through experience, that Taureans usually have quite deep and melodious voices.

Each sign has its own strengths and weaknesses. There are certain foods that are truly marvellous for promoting good health in each sign, and I'll be describing those.

What I had never anticipated early on in my psychic career was that the sign of the zodiac could affect the looks of each individual. Naturally, the looks and body shape of biological parents are the biggest determining factor. It would be stupid to ignore something so obvious. But allowing for that, each sign still assigns something special and individual to everyone. Leos really do have large and beautiful eyes. Geminians really do have light, pleasing and rapid voices.

The greatest lesson I have had is in recognising the role of stress in each person's life. When someone phones in to the radio show to ask a question of me, I can also register the level of stress the caller is experiencing. Sometimes the voice is low and weary, and I form a picture in my mind of someone who has carried so great a load in life that they can barely function adequately, and have lost the capacity to work out solutions to problems. One woman caller who was deeply concerned about the state of her relationship had a voice that crackled with so much stress that I doubted her ability to stay on the line without breaking down and weeping.

But each sign has its own stress-busting secrets, and I am going to share with you what those secrets are.

It is so obvious that I don't really suppose I need to say it, but I'll do it anyway. Health is wealth! Without good mental and physical health, life is a hard and difficult business. I recall one woman who came to my office for a reading. She had been quite snappy on the phone and didn't seem able to concentrate when she was being given directions to get to the office, so as the note on my desk informed me, I felt she might either be late or not turn up. But she did arrive, only a few minutes late with a deeply frowning expression, a down-turned mouth and a slow walk. I was psychically aware that her facial expression was not because of bad temper but because she was in deep chronic pain. I could feel that she was trapped in a vicious circle; the more she reached out to others for help and sympathy, the more bad-tempered she looked, the more her voice whined (the whining voice is a subconscious repetition of a childish voice, telling the listener that the adult is really a child and needs help and care) thus turning people away from her.

But it's very hard to look pretty, attractive and appealing when the body is in pain and the mind so stressed that rational conversation is an impossibility.

Eventually the woman was able to relax and began to speak about the dreadful things occurring in her life, and the complete lack of support she received from family members. She felt alone in her pain, and that made it a tough and lonely place.

Another regular client who began her career with youthful joy and enthusiasm became so overcome with the stress of it that she, within eight years, had aged dramatically, had a permanent headache, and developed a nervous twitch. Stress had made her incapable of leaving the job. The more stressed she became, the harder she worked to get on top of a situation in which she couldn't win. Thankfully, she did eventually leave and took up a different career, and got her happy young life back.

I do recognise the role of stress in life and have seen over and over again what a huge difference the relief from stress makes to each person. But I am still reluctant to link stress to physical disease. It's bad enough to get cancer or suffer from chronic back pain, but it's even harder if someone with half-baked ideas and no medical expertise whatsoever tells you that somehow it's your own fault, because you brought it on yourself by being stressed.

I believe stress wears down the immune system so that underlying physical conditions surface, and try to have a field day with the body. Some signs are better than others at coping with stress. But there is stress help for every sign of the zodiac.

The Zodiac And The Body

Below is a list of the signs of the zodiac and the parts of the body they are associated with.

GEMINI rules the shoulders, the arms, the hands and the lungs.

CANCER rules the breasts and stomach.

ARIES rules the head and the face.

AQUARIUS rules the circulatory system and from the knees down; the calves, shins and ankles.

PISCES rules the feet and toes, and the mucous membranes.

TAURUS rules the throat, vocal glands, neck, tonsils and tongue.

VIRGO rules the nervous system and the intestine.

LEO rules the spine and the heart.

SCORPIO rules the sexual organs.

LIBRA rules the kidneys, lower back and the bottom.

CAPRICORN rules the bones, joints, knees and teeth.

SAGITTARIUS rules the hips, thighs and liver.

There is a link between the parts of the body governed by each sign and the predominant characteristic of each sign. I'll take you through each one.

CANCER has always been associated with nurturing and motherhood. Of course, Cancerian woman doesn't have the monopoly on motherhood, or make a better mother than any other sign. But Cancer often defines the whole life by the motherhood role. The parts of the body — the stomach and breasts — governed by Cancer symbolise nourishment and motherhood. Cancer is an emotional sign, a water sign, delicately balanced. Although Cancer woman is a great cook and will feed her family banquet-style, she has a delicate stomach and often can't eat rich food. When she is tense or strained emotionally, she gets stomach problems. Flatulence is a real problem and her wind pains are often excruciating. When Cancer woman gets indigestion she is practically incapacitated by it. When she is upset, she often feels physically sick.

If she is stuck in a job she hates, or an emotional situation that becomes intolerable, she may even get stomach ulcers. Gall bladder problems and gastritis are often experienced. Cancerian women enjoy their wine – what water sign doesn't? – but wine, or any alcohol, is not well tolerated by that delicate Cancerian stomach.

Later, if weight does go on, then the stomach and breasts are the first to fill out.

GEMINI is another nervous sign, but the bodily reaction is different. Gemini governs the shoulders, arms, hands and lungs. Gemini also rules the nerves and this makes Geminians a very excitable and highly-strung sign. I've found that the Gemini state of mind has a lot to do with health. When Geminians get anxious and nervous, they can get physically sick. They sometimes seem a bit unstable. It doesn't last; as soon as they calm down, or learn a meditation technique, they calm down and control the body. Geminians are quite vulnerable to bouts of asthma, chest infections and colds. Gemini often gets pain, for no apparent reason, across the shoulders and down the arms. The hands, which are often beautiful and expressive, seem to get damaged and slightly injured in day-to-day activity more often than with other signs. Gemini should avoid working with the hands.

But ARIES does work with the hands; such work is good for them. Aries rules the head and face, thinks a great deal, and is very shrewd in thought and instinct. Aries also has oceans of common sense. But they suffer headaches and migraines more often than other signs. I've also seen Arians quite incapacitated by sinus problems. But whether large or small, Arians have beautiful and well co-ordinated muscles, walk well, and make superb dancers and athletes.

TAURUS is not so well known for athletic skill. The Taurean speciality is that marvellous voice and exquisite palate. Taureans love good food. Their taste buds are so keenly developed that they make natural wine-tasters. Taurus, taking the most minute sip of soup, can tell the chef instantly what needs to be added to make it more delicious.

Even in early childhood, Taureans suffer from throat problems; tonsillitis, laryngitis, swollen glands and stiff necks. They seem to get colds very often. This goes on until adulthood. Even when Taurean children have their tonsils out, they go on getting sore throats. Taurus likes food and isn't that mad about exercise, so weight gain can be a problem even in early adulthood.

LEO is another food lover of the zodiac. But Leo doesn't often gain weight as easily as Taurus. Leo is an athletic, supple sign. Leo rules the back and heart. There is an emotional link here. Leo has a lot of courage — that emotion is associated with the back — and a very warm heart. Most Leos have a robust body and a courageous attitude to life. They are well co-ordinated and make supple dancers and sports people.

There is so much vitality radiating from Leo, both mentally and physically, that it's infectious. Leo is used to having a lot of energy and sometimes carries on at forty in exactly the same way as they did at twenty. Many can, energy undiminished, but it's wiser to slow down a bit, otherwise pains and strains show around the back and heart. I'm not scare mongering here about heart problems! Leo is known to be a long-living sign. It is a really feisty fire sign.

PISCES is not quite the opposite of Leo, but as a water sign is very different. Leo and Pisces do share a love of dancing, and show a real flair turning this enjoyable pastime into an art form. Not surprising, since Pisces governs the feet and toes. Pisceans should look for modelling work where feet have to be displayed, because they really do have the most beautiful feet, whether they are long and shapely or cute and small. But they can also get corns and bunions and need to wear sensible shoes. Not an appealing idea, since Pisceans love their glamorous image and high fashion!

This is a sensitive and emotional sign and bad health is very often linked to a sensitive emotional state. Their sense of taste and smell is acute too, and they are vulnerable to colds, sinus trouble and retaining water. Pisces likes late party hours and free flowing wine, but really can't handle either.

Neither can ✥ **SAGITTARIUS**, although they rarely admit it. Sagittarius governs the hips, thighs and liver. If Sagittarius drinks alcohol, it instantly affects the liver, making Sagittarius fatigued and irritable.

There are lots of pains and aches in the hips and thighs from sciatica, gout and hip-disease. Sometimes Sagittarius suffers lameness. Physical activity is a must for Sagittarians. Most Sagittarians enjoy physical activity, but it must be a long term practice or they'll get ill.

CAPRICORN can't handle too much alcohol either; it affects their skin. Capricorn rules the bones, and most Capricorns have the most beautiful bone structure. But they do get bone problems — knees especially — and rheumatism, arthritis and stiff joints are other problems they endure. Capricorn is also vulnerable to problems with teeth, sensitive skin, gall-bladder problems and overwork.

Capricorn thinks that overwork is a virtue. It isn't. It makes them drive their bodies too hard, sitting at a desk or in the car for too-long periods, aggravating bone and joint problems. Meals are skipped and one gigantic one is eaten too late at night. This is not a good recipe for good health. Yet, like Leo and Sagittarius, Capricorn is known to enjoy a long life.

AQUARIUS is a strong, mainly healthy sign too. Like Capricorn, they are more mentally than physically active, but show the effects of this in different ways. Calves, shins and ankles (ruled by Aquarius) are usually slender and beautifully shaped. They have a strong, healthy and energetic way of walking, which is good for them as they can tend to put on weight easily. Because they have such a mentally active lifestyle and are always involved in some project or another, they tend to skip meals, even snacking on the run between one activity and another. There can be circulation problems, hardening of the arteries, anaemia and low blood pressure. But their vitality remains undimmed.

SCORPIO is another sign full of vitality. Scorpios have tremendous energy and a permanently switched on imagination. The sign rules the sexual organs and Scorpios often get infections of the sexual organs. There can be skin problems on the genitals, cystitis and urinary tract infections. Scorpios are also susceptible to sexually transmitted diseases. But this sign is also highly emotional and it is often suggested that either strong emotion, or even guilt, can make Scorpio more prone to problems in the sexual area.

As a natural bonus, Scorpio has the most powerful recuperative abilities in the zodiac. I have seen Scorpios looking virtually at death's door one day, and looking almost completely recovered the next.

But these problems aren't necessarily frequent, as Scorpio usually enjoys good health.

LIBRA normally enjoys good health too. The sign rules the kidneys, lower back and buttocks. Librans have fine skin and good features but can be prone to skin blemishes, especially when they overwork. The lower back gives problems if Libra puts in too many work hours without rest and exercise breaks. Libra is prone to kidney ailments more than other signs.

Good relationships are crucial to Libra's sense of well-being. If a relationship is unbalanced, then Libra suffers throat problems, skin blemishes, back pain and some kidney problems. Often, if Libra addresses the imbalance in a relationship, they prepare the body better for healing and responding to treatment. An excellent health adviser for Libra is Virgo.

VIRGO is very knowledgeable in all health matters. Virgo worries a lot about health. The sign rules the nervous system and intestines. Sometimes Virgo can literally worry itself sick. They get nervous or anxious about something and dwell on the problem, turning inwards into their own body. The intestine suffers and food doesn't get assimilated into their body easily.

Indigestion results, with wind and flatulence causing pain and problems. There can be liver and bowel problems, and also colitis. Rich or highly spiced food, whilst tasting delicious at the time, can leave poor old Virgo suffering for hours afterwards.

But for every health ailment, in each of the signs, there is astrological help on hand and some really sound advice.

Diet

————

S omeone once said that you are what you eat. It's also true that you are what you don't eat. Each sign of the zodiac has a proneness to different health problems. Fortunately, each sign has some firm dietary do's and don'ts which can be very helpful.

♍ **VIRGO** really does seem to suffer a lot. If the food taken in can't be dealt with, then suffering is bound to occur on a daily basis. Fatigue and constipation are by-products of the system not being able to handle food. Virgo needs lots of leafy green vegetables, whole wheat and whole grain breads, oats, cheese, oranges, bananas and lemons. Lean beef and lamb are good with brown rice, yoghurt, eggs and cottage cheese. Honey and lemon are great for the skin and soothing to the stomach.

♋ **CANCER**, like Virgo, suffers stomach problems and also needs to eat lots of lean protein, fresh vegetables, fresh fruit, milk, cheese, lettuce and tomatoes and loads of fish on a daily basis. Fish at least two or three times a week is a Cancerian must. Egg whites are soothing and good for the Cancerian system. But Cancer should steer clear of spicy foods, very highly seasoned foods, and cut down on the sweets. Milky drinks or desserts are therapeutic for the Cancerian system.

ARIES should drink lots of milk, too. It's good for their teeth and bones. Aries also needs to include tomatoes, beans, brown rice and lentils, walnuts, olives, onions and cauliflower in the diet. More Aries good foods are cucumber, spinach, broccoli, bananas and apricots. Aries should cut down on alcohol and drink plenty of water.

TAURUS also needs to drink plenty of water to flush out the system. Asparagus, beetroot, cauliflower and spinach are really good for Taureans. So are cucumbers, onions, nuts and cranberry juice. That Taurean love of good food can be satisfied with fresh fish, seafood, eggs, liver, kidney beans and masses of fresh fruit and vegetables. But avoid too much heavy, rich food, because it doesn't like the Taurean system.

Fortunately for **GEMINI**, they don't like loads of heavy, rich food. Gemini ideally works well with four or five small meals a day. They need asparagus, green beans, celery, tomatoes, spinach, lettuce and cauliflower. Fish, milk and cheese keep Gemini healthy as does a lot of salad and vegetables, and fish and rice. Grapefruit, either juiced or whole and orange either juiced or whole, is good too.

Gemini should try to avoid one of their great loves — junk food — as often as possible. This is hard, but it gets easier when Gemini begins to feel a lot more energetic as a result. When Gemini isn't snacking on junk food, this sign has a natural instinct to go for a good diet, because Gemini is naturally attracted to food that is good for them and suits the system. They also give good dietary advice to other signs. What Gemini has to say about diet is well worth hearing.

PISCES might lend an ear to Geminian advice and top up on all the foods they need to combat anaemia and low blood pressure, getting as much liver, lean beef and lamb into them as possible. Unless of course they are one of the ten per cent of vegetarians in the country. In that case they should go for kidney beans, whole grain cereals, dried beans, barley, spinach, onions, and lettuce, and include raisins, fish, dates, eggs, apricots, peaches, grapes, apples and oranges in as many meals as possible.

Definitely cut down on salt — it bloats — and coffee, and drink hot water with a good dash of lemon juice. Great for Pisceans.

Although **AQUARIUS** is not a water sign, Aquarians should also eat loads of fish, especially lobster and tuna. Lots and lots of vegetables like spinach, celery, cabbage, lettuce and radishes are also good. Lentils are good for Aquarians, as is chicken and wholegrain bread. Yoghurt and cheese with carrots, peppers and tomatoes are necessary, and for dessert, strawberries, pineapple, figs and dates. Brown rice is wholesome and entirely necessary.

Aquarius loves coffee but should cut down, as it makes them very nervous.

🦁 **LEO** is not a nervous sign on the face of it, but doesn't always have the confidence needed. Often this comes from not being happy with their diet. Leo needs to be happy with what is eaten. Wholewheat bread with beef, lamb, chicken, liver and lots and lots of fresh green vegetables and salad foods is always best. Yoghurt and raisins are a favourite with Leos, and they like honey and fruits to soothe the sweet tooth. They have to cut down on the foods that make them fat and eventually uncomfortable.

🐐 **CAPRICORN** can take a leaf – literally – from the Leo diet book, as they also have to cut down on fatty foods. Capricorn needs lots of celery, cabbage, spinach, broccoli, peas (notice how many greens), potatoes, nuts and brown rice. Raw salads and eggs, yoghurts with a lot of lean meat, fish and cheese are advised. Loads of milk and milky drinks are a soothing and nutritious addition to the Capricorn diet, ensuring that Capricorn keeps those youthful looks.

Capricorn has a very set diet and should try to vary it a bit. As a treat they should eat peaches, grapes and apples, but avoid fatty foods.

If 🦂 **SCORPIO** could be persuaded to eat all the fruits Capricorn eats, they would be much happier emotionally. Emotional well-being is essential to Scorpio. But so is the need for a diet high in protein, including a lot of sea food, cheese, wholegrain and lentils. A soup-blend of lentils, onions, tomatoes and nuts is a wonderful restorer and tonic. A large salad of onions, tomatoes, radishes and cottage cheese stimulates the Scorpio appetite. Potatoes or brown rice is good, followed by bananas, apples and pineapples. Scorpio should avoid large meals, especially in the evening. Four small meals a day is ideal, and in between, Scorpio should take flat water and a few glasses of tomato juice.

SAGITTARIUS should also go for juices, either fruit or vegetable. A juicer would do so much for Sagittarian health. Juicing up the celery, apple and carrot necessary to Sagittarius and drinking it down would give an instant energy boost. Sagittarius thrives on raw salads of cabbage, lettuce, onions, carrots, green peppers, parsnips and turnip. Sagittarius also needs lots of lean protein in the form of lamb, beef and cheese. Brown rice with peas and lentil soup have the kind of flavour that appeal to the Sagittarian palate, especially if spiced with chilli and lots of tomatoes, tomato puree and eggs. Ideally, a large omelette folded around cheese and tomatoes is a great Sagittarian snack.

Four or five small meals a day suit Sagittarians, and if they avoid fats, gravies, cream and butter, and include lots of water and fruit in the diet, they are quite happy.

LIBRA and Sagittarius should get together over the diet issue because the same diet suits both. The best Libran health aid is plenty of sleep. Libra is lucky in liking fresh natural foods like strawberries, apples, carrots, spinach, beetroot, tomatoes, radishes and salads. Librans also enjoy seafood and chicken, as well as yoghurt and cottage cheese. They avoid eating too much ham, pork and bacon, liking instead foods and liquids that naturally flush out the kidneys. Librans should avoid the rich foods and go for the foods and all those fruit juices they love.

Librans are wise about diet and probably avoid all the things that are bad for them, like carbonated drinks, alcohol and chocolates.

Libra has such an intuitive knowledge of the diet suited to each individual that they are one of the best dieticians in the zodiac.

YOUR STAR SIGN AND YOUR LOOKS

Of course, your looks are inherited from your parents. Colouring, build and health predispositions are all in the gene pool you came into the world with. But your sign of the zodiac gives you the little bit extra that makes you different. If it wasn't for that, every child of the two biological parents would be quite similar. Here is what makes you that little bit special in the way you look.

✵ **SAGITTARIUS** is special because no matter what they do or don't do about diet or exercise, they always seem to have a healthy complexion and a strong, mobile body. The face is often long, with a straight and prominent nose. The eyes seem to take in the world around them and then home in on the person before them, taking a deep and very friendly interest. The mouth is wide and broadens into an infectious grin when talking to another person. That grin is infectious and draws people into the fun world of this appealing and outgoing fire sign.

✺ **CANCER** is almost the opposite in body structure and facial characteristics. Cancerians are physically more rounded people. Cancerians have, as a rule, lovely eyes set wide apart. The expression is usually one of gentle concern. The head of hair is plentiful but often fine and light in texture. Movements are quite slow and measured. There is a very reassuring presence about this very feminine individual.

Side by side, even if closely related, the signs of Cancer and Virgo have very marked differences.

♍ **VIRGO** is usually noticeably thinner than Cancer. Where Cancer might have a light complexion, Virgo is noticeably darker. The face is an almost classical oval shape, with a high forehead and a long, and well-defined nose. The chin can often be quite pointed. Elegance is the key feature of Virgo woman.

A well-defined face also characterises ♒ **AQUARIUS**, who always seem light, yet not unsubstantial, people. They move firmly but lightly, using their long, athletic body with a certain grace and balance. The face is clear and open looking. 'Clear' is the operative word, as Aquarius gets through the teen years without the spots and blemishes that plague most young people.

Like Aquarius, ♎ **LIBRA** is an air sign, but does get the teen skin blemishes. Blemished or not, very little can dim Libran good looks. The face is a regular oval, the eyes wide and friendly, the walk lithe and graceful. It's no wonder that so many models come from this sign, or that Libra even into advanced years can turn heads as they tread lightly and gracefully down the street. Walking with long free flowing steps is the Libran speciality. Libra is definitely one of the prettiest signs of the zodiac. Quite often, Libran women have long backs and long legs with oval faces and large angelic eyes. Whether washing dishes or putting on rings, the hands are graceful and beautifully shaped. That Libran smile wins and breaks hearts.

ARIES moves as quickly as Libra, but not as lightly. Aries moves with speed and determination, as though permanently on a mission. The arms swing in the walk, as though on military parade. Arians always manage to appear taller than they actually are. The carriage is upright, definite. The face is quite triangular, with wide set, alert eyes and a pointed chin. Aries often has a serious expression. But that Arian smile, when it appears, disarms and charms the world.

SCORPIO is a charmer too, but doesn't set out to be that. There is a sense of concentrated power in the Scorpio frame. The build is fairly athletic and Scorpios often have hands that are a little larger than usual. Facial features are well formed, the mouth sensuous. But those Scorpio eyes are quite unforgettable. There is something in that look that captivates and hypnotises. Once a Scorpio woman has held a man in her gorgeous gaze he will never, ever forget her.

LEO women have lovely eyes too. But those eyes look out on the world from beneath strongly marked eyebrows. The Leo eyes sometimes look angry — they actually aren't, just interested in the world. Leo features are strong and the hair appears thick, full and when swept back off the face, magnificent. The walk is energetic and free flowing, the body strong, attractive and athletic. Whether tall or short, fat or thin, the Leo, from a very early age, has an air of command about them that draws instant attention.

GEMINI isn't an attention seeker, but even tiny or young Geminis have a habit of looking all around the room, or street, or party, as though seeking out a friend to talk to. The most noticeable thing about Gemini is the movement. They walk quickly, the mobile mouth rarely stops moving, the hands are used to gesticulate in speaking, the chuckle is infectious. Gemini women often have perfect figures with bust and hips the same size, and even when putting on weight this almost perfect balance is maintained. Most noticeably, the hairline usually starts well back, leaving the Gemini forehead exposed and seeming large and well rounded. The eyes always have a most attractive quality.

Taurean eyes have that attractive quality too. But **TAURUS** seems broader than Gemini. The body is voluptuous, the face broader, with a wide and generous mouth. The eyes are wide and full and the expression keenly interested. Taurus has the knack of sudden stillness. When talking with another person, the Taurean sometimes becomes completely immobile, giving the whole of that concentrated Taurean attention to whom so ever is speaking. It is a very attractive quality. Even when weight goes on, Taurean women never quite lose those slim hips or that energetic walk.

The Piscean smile is lovely. It has a childlike quality. ♓ **PISCES** has a rounded shape about the hips and bottom. Even when losing weight or exercising, the shape remains the same. Like Libra, Pisceans have an angelic face. The forehead is high and round, the eyes full, sometimes sleepy looking, the lips small and full, the chin round and soft. Those eyes are always expressive, sometimes soulful, other times full of mischief. But always the Pisces face has that childlike appeal that goes on winning hearts well into old age.

The ♑ **CAPRICORN** woman is attractive too, but in a very different way to Pisces. Capricorn woman has strong, well-defined features. The jaw is firm, the cheekbones clearly defined and often high. The mouth is firm and straight. The eyes often don't show much emotion. The whole appearance is commanding and magnetic. The body movements are elegant. Capricorns are often mistaken for royalty, or, at least, the very rich. But when Capricorn does smile, the whole room lights up. When Miss Capricorn is amused, she has a habit of throwing her head back and allowing that deep throaty chuckle to float infectiously around the place.

STRESS-BUSTING SECRETS

———

We need a certain amount of healthy stress in our lives, otherwise we wouldn't get much done. Healthy stress drives a person to study for that examination, or put that bill on top of the pile ready for payment, or makes each person put in the extra effort to be on time for an appointment, or do that job particularly well.

Stress is healthy and necessary when it helps us prioritise tasks so that something important is given extra emphasis. This special emphasis needed to get something done is usually of a temporary nature. When the appointment is kept or the task completed, that extra effort is no longer needed. Some people demand extra attention; this emphasis needed in dealing with the person is usually temporary too. Say, if a sick child has to be nursed; the extra attention and emphasis end as the child gets better. A partner or friend may need attention because something out of the ordinary happened that day. This too involves temporary stress. An interview might be coming up. This meeting is important, out of the ordinary, and needs concentration in getting ready for it, thinking about it, finding out where the interview is taking place, anticipating the questions and answers, preparing to meet a total stranger. All of this can bring stress.

Most of us can associate with the stress of driving. Driving in difficult or chaotic conditions requires extra emphasis on motoring skills and full concentration. Putting the senses on full alert is draining and fatiguing. It makes concentration on anything else very difficult. But here, as from time to time in other situations, temporary stress is necessary. It makes us focus.

What is difficult is when this stressful condition lasts. What makes it nightmarish is when there is no time limit to it. If the friend, spouse or family member arrives in every day with some fresh drama or odd mood, it means that every day is a stressful day. If the driving conditions are permanently difficult or chaotic, then stress exists every day. If the work is constantly demanding and deadlines always have to be met, and there is no support, then stress is a permanent factor of life.

Stress needs to be rested. But if a woman works outside the home and has to come home and start working again, she needs to keep her stress levels up to cope with cooking, supervising homework — if there are school going children — and then make arrangements for the next day. If she has a co-operative partner, life is much easier and the burdens are shared. But if that partner arrives home and brings in a fresh set of demands on her time and emotions, the stress is not eased. She needs to bring attention and emphasis into that situation too.

As I have already said, stress is naturally fatiguing; it needs to be switched off regularly. Each sign of the zodiac has its own special ways of coping with stress.

Use those skills; they are vital to coping and surviving. Stress can fatigue, drain and age. But I can show you now what the stress busting secrets are in each sign of the zodiac.

≈ PISCES woman needs quiet — absolute silence — for twenty minutes after dealing with a stressful situation. If possible, after a long stressful day, try to switch off the mind in a quiet place, be alone, preferably in the dark and warmth, and ideally in bed. It works wonders. Daydreaming is essential for Pisceans. In the dark, quiet and warmth, let your mind free to have its favourite day dream. It can work wonders and leave the mind and body deeply relaxed and refreshed.

✺ SAGITTARIUS need some physical activity and can't or won't allow themselves space to day dream. Sagittarius responds well to a long walk or a swim. After a stressful day or encounter, get off the bus a stop early and walk the rest of the way home. Or if there has been a stressful encounter at home or work, physically get out of the place and walk around the block. This has an instant and calming effect on the mind and body.

Walking is also good for ♒ AQUARIUS. Stress raises the anger levels in Aquarians. They snap and jump. Much better to remove themselves from the situation and walk. Even better to take a Walkman and listen to the news. Other peoples' problems are absorbing and take the busy Aquarian's mind off the problem at hand.

🐐 **CAPRICORN,** would do well to take up walking like this, but they don't do much of it; they are too busy. Capricorn is best advised to stop — dead — don't even think about working when stressed. It may not be the actual work that stresses Capricorn out, but the sheer amount of it does. It doesn't leave time for dealing with anything else. Climb into a hot soapy bath, or get under a hot steamy shower for ten minutes. Let that body stop all activity and the mind switch off for ten minutes. This one really works for Capricorn woman.

🐏 **ARIES** is a high activity sign too, and in busting stress, a little pleasant activity is the order of the day. Try handling wood. Try actual woodwork. If that can't be managed, sand down a piece of wood, paint it, varnish it. No? Can't do it? Then get duster out and polish some wood. Do it slowly, thoroughly, methodically, and after ten or fifteen minutes, Arian stress is well and truly lowered.

Wood works well for 🐂 **TAURUS,** but food is even better. Sit down, alone, with a cook book and find a lovely recipe for a favourite meal. Taurus is a great cook and likes thinking about food, planning menus and, of course, eating it. If Taurus is on a diet, chop up a couple of sticks of celery, an apple, and some bits of cheese. Mix it all together in a bowl. Drizzle over a teaspoon of olive oil. Eat slowly, savouring each mouthful. The very act of handling food, chopping it, arranging it and eating it is one of the best stress busters for Taurus.

That wouldn't work for ♊ **GEMINI**. Food is the last thing on her mind when she's stressed. Gemini needs to talk it out. Find the calmest, quietest person you can think of, Gemini woman, and talk to her. Let out all that stress and anger. When Gemini is stressed, it makes her angry. Talking gets everything out and a calm friend helps bring the temperature down, bringing perspective to that stressful situation.

Talking would help ♋ **CANCER** woman, but she often finds it difficult to talk when stressed. There is often a thumping headache and sometimes blood pressure rises. A long swim helps. If that isn't possible, have a relaxation tape standing by. Put it on and allow the mind and body to relax, listening to a deeply soothing and calming voice. It works. Try it!

Listening soothes ♏ **SCORPIO**, but music is often more effective than the human voice, unless it's someone singing. Music has great power over the Scorpio spirit. It calms the mind and lifts the spirits. If sad music makes the Scorpio cry a bit, even better. But follow it up with something energising and cheerful.

Cheering up works well for ♌ **LEO** when trying to reduce stress. Leo woman often gets back pain or headaches when stressed, and usually can't bear the sight or sound of another person around. Leo needs to be alone to de-stress. She needs to take out a holiday brochure and plan that dream holiday (even if the reality is an impossibility) on a long, white, sandy beach, beneath a sun-drenched, deep blue sky, where she can dip in and out of warm water and listen to the gentle lapping of waves. This one never fails for Leo.

This would work for ♍ **VIRGO** woman too, if only she allowed her practical mind to dwell on such bliss. But she is practical to the last and is usually worried for good reason. A big cup of calming herbal tea, taken out of doors, works well. When stressed, Virgo woman needs to get out of doors and connect with nature. The sky, sun, wind or rain ground her, calm her, and give her back that healthy calm that is vital to her survival.

Calm is second nature to ♎ **LIBRA** woman and she is least likely to suffer prolonged stress. What she needs when stressed is a long hug. Find your favourite person to give you a warm and reassuring hug, Libra woman. It works! Nobody around? Hug a pillow, a teddy bear, anything soft and warm, and just feel all that tension easing away.

Of course, hugging works for everyone. Give yourself a hug, and do it often, no matter what sign of the zodiac you are. You deserve it because you are a special and lovely person who deserves the very best life has to offer.